ALSO BY FALL RIVER HISTORICAL SOCIETY PRESS

Women at Work: An Oral History of Working Class Women in Fall River, Massachusetts, 1920 to 1970 (2017)

❦

Parallel Lives: A Social History of Lizzie A. Borden and Her Fall River (2011)

❦

The Commonwealth of Massachussetts vs. Lizzie A. Borden: The Knowlton Papers, 1892-1893 (1994)

❦

∽ **DISCOURSES ON HISTORY SERIES** ∽
NUMBER 1

ANTI-SLAVERY DAYS IN FALL RIVER
AND THE
OPERATION OF THE UNDERGROUND RAILROAD

by
Edward Stowe Adams
(1856-1948)

*With a supplement pertaining to Rev. Joshua Young
and "The Funeral of John Brown"*

FALL RIVER HISTORICAL SOCIETY

Edited and annotated by Michael Martins and Dennis A. Binette

FALL RIVER
HISTORICAL SOCIETY
PRESS

Fall River Historical Society Press
451 Rock Street
Fall River, MA 02720
fallriverhistorical.org
(508) 679-1071

For information, write us at Fall River Historical Society,
451 Rock Street, Fall River, MA 02720.

LIBRARY OF CONGRESS CONTROL NUMBER: 2017935986

ISBN-10: 0-9641248-5-8
ISBN-13: 978-0-96-412485-1

Printed in the United States of America on acid-free paper.

Book and cover design by Stefani Koorey, PearTree Press, Fall River, MA

Front cover: "Edmund Commander <u>before</u> your boxes came."

ANTI-SLAVERY DAYS IN FALL RIVER
AND THE
OPERATION OF THE UNDERGROUND RAILROAD

CONTENTS

CONTENTS

List of Illustrations — ix
Introduction to Discourses on History — xiii
About the Author — xvii
Editors' Note — xxi

Anti-Slavery Days in Fall River and the Operation of the Underground Railroad — 1

Author's Notes — 81

Supplement
Rev. Joshua Young and *"The Funeral of John Brown"* — 87

Bibliography — 121
About the Fall River Historical Society — 125
Acknowledgments — 129
Index — 131

LIST OF ILLUSTRATIONS

Fig.		Page
1	Edward Stowe Adams.	xvi
2	"Bills of Sale of slaves."	3
3	Arnold Buffum, 1826. *From a portrait by George Freeman (England, 1789-1868).*	4
4	Masthead from William Lloyd Garrison's abolitionist newspaper, *The Liberator.*	9
5	William Henry Hawkins. *Albert L. Ward, Fall River.*	11
6	"View of the Great Fire in Fall River, July 2, 1843." *Lithograph by George Endicott of New York, from an engraving by textile artist Edward Ruggles.*	12
7	"View of Fall River Looking South Down Main Street," 1839. *Woodcut, John Warner Barber,* Massachusetts Historical Collections.	13
8	Mrs. William Buffington Chace, née Elizabeth Buffum.	14
9	The home of Nathaniel B. Borden.	18
10	Friend William Hill.	19
11	Louisa Buffum, later Mrs. William Mowry Hawes, circa 1857. *Anthony Chace, Fall River.*	20
12	The "stone mansion" built for Andrew Robeson Jr.	21
13	William Barnabas Canedy residence.	22
14	Residence of Mr. & Mrs. William Buffington Chace.	23
15	Robert Adams.	25
16	Anthony Burns. *Illustration drawn by Charles A. Barry, portrait after a daguerreotype by James Adams Whipple and James Wallace Black, Commercial Photographers, Boston, Massachusetts; Printed by R. M. Edwards, Boston, 1855.*	27

Fig.		Page
17	Albion King Slade.	28
18	Mrs. Albion King Slade, née Mary Bridge Canedy.	28
19	Mrs. Reverend Nehemiah Gorham Lovell, née Lucy Buffum.	30
20	Abraham Bowen residence.	32
21	Nathaniel Briggs Borden. *Engraving by J. W. Lewis & Company, Philadelphia, Pennsylvania.*	33
22	Reverend Asa Bronson. *Gay's Gallery of Art, Fall River, Massachusetts.*	33
23	James Ford, Esq. *Anthony Chace, Fall River, Massachusetts.*	34
24	Reverend Orin Fowler.	35
25	The Hutchinson Family Singers, 1843. *Engraving by G. & W. Endicott, Beekman Street, New York, New York.*	37
26	"Get Off The Track!" sheet music, 1844. *Published by Henry Prentiss, 33 Court Street, Boston, Massachusetts.*	38
27	"An illustration from Harriet Beecher Stowe's *Uncle Tom's Cabin*, published in 1852."	41
28	Andrew Robeson, Jr.	42
29	Dr. Foster Hooper.	42
30	Dr. James Mott Aldrich. *Albert L. Ward, Fall River, Massachusetts.*	42
31	Hon. Dr. Robert Thompson Davis. *Albert L. Ward, Fall River, Massachusetts.*	42
32	John Brown, abolitionist, an engraving after an 1859 photograph.	44
33	Dr. Phineas Washington Leland. *Engraving by F. T. Stuart, Boston, Massachusetts.*	46
34	Town Hall and Market Building.	51
35	"Members of the Young Men's Republican Club of Fall River, Massachusetts."	52
36	Reverend Peter Britton Haughwout.	53
37	Company F, 26th Regiment Massachusetts Volunteer Infantry. *George M. Carlisle, Fall River, Massachusetts.*	55
38	Eunice Hathaway (Congdon) Dixon.	56

Fig.		Page
39	Mrs. Robert Adams, née Lydia Ann Stowe.	58
40	"Edmund Commander <u>before</u> your boxes came."	62
41	"Edmund Commander <u>after</u> your boxes came."	63
42	Quaker Meeting House, Fall River, Massachusetts.	64
43	"The Effects of the Proclamation: Freed Negros Coming into Our Lines at New Bern, North Carolina." *Harper's Weekly, Vol. VII, No. 321, February 21, 1863.*	67
44	Edward Stowe Adams, 1873. *Gay's Gallery of Art, Fall River, Massachusetts.*	68
45	James Ford, Esq.	68
46	Reverend John Westall. *Engraving by E. G. William & Brother, New York, New York.*	68
47	Anne Chaloner Graves Canedy.	71
48	Aerial view of Fall River, Massachusetts, looking north, late 1860s.	73
49	Azariah Shove Tripp.	74
50	Sojourner Truth.	78
51	Frederick Douglass.	79
52	Rev. Joshua Young; *Notman Photo Company, Boston and Cambridge, Massachusetts.*	86
53	Mrs. Rev. Joshua Young; *The Litchfield Studio, Arlington, Massachusetts.*	89
54	Unitarian Church, Fall River, Massachusetts; *Fall River Illustrated, H. R. Page & Company, Chicago, Illinois, 1891.*	90
55	First Parish Unitarian Church, Groton, Massachusetts.	91
56	Rev. and Mrs. Young in their residence.	91
57	Letter to Rev. Young from Annie (Brown) Adams, May 19, 1897.	110
58	Letter to Rev. Young from Annie (Brown) Adams, March 5, 1899.	113
59	Letter to Rev. Young from Ruth (Brown) Thompson, March 17, 1899.	116

INTRODUCTION TO
DISCOURSES ON HISTORY

At the time of its incorporation in 1921, and for the half century that followed, it was customary for members of the Fall River Historical Society to research papers for presentation at the organization's meetings. Traditionally, copies of these manuscripts were deposited at the Society, with the intention that they be made available to researchers, and a select few were serialized, in part, in local newspapers.

Not all of the lectures were illustrated at the time of their original presentation. The earliest of those that was accompanied by images featured black-and-white glass lantern slides, usually shown at the culmination of the lecture, while those of later date included slides in vivid Kodachrome. Fortunately, many of these images were deposited at the Historical Society, along with the original manuscripts.

In 1927, the organization published *Fall River Historical Society: Proceedings of the Society from Its Organization in 1921 to August, 1926*, which contained a selection of ten "papers on local subjects," and a comprehensive list of all of the speakers and topics presented as of that date. The volume was not illustrated, excepting one photograph of the Market Building and Town Hall, a solid Greek revival style building erected in 1845 of native granite. If the original intent was to publish additional volumes, this never came to fruition.

In subsequent years, the collection of papers amassed by the organization grew accordingly; topics varied widely, encompassing all manner of subject matter, with the common thread being the history of Fall River and its environs. This thematic variety furnishes a richly diverse tapestry, with subjects ranging from Native Americans to intrepid gold-seeking "Forty-Niners," from transportation in all its forms to industry of myriad types, or from memories of languid "Golden Summers" to the reminiscences of a policewoman, serving at a time when few women ventured into the field.

And what of the writers? Many individuals possessed superior literary skills and were methodical in research and writing, while others, somewhat less eloquent, nonetheless made the attempt, presenting papers on subjects that held their particular interest. The diverse personalities of the writers oftentimes come to the fore: There were those who pontificated, and others that rambled; some were witty, and others dry; and if truth be told, a few produced manuscripts that were accurately described by the transcriber of these papers as quintessential "yawners."

Among the presenters were brilliant conversationalists, and those with keen, descriptive memories; their papers are peppered with fascinating anecdotes, and references to individuals referred to by diminutives of their given names that would otherwise have been lost to history. So, too, were there academics, attorneys, ministers, physicians, and businessmen, whose oratory characteristically reflected their education and professions: the first lectured; the second deliberated; the third preached; the fourth delivered clinical narrative; and the last, board-room discourse or gentlemen's club banter.

Spinsters, of which there were several, often reflected through the lenses of proverbial rose-colored glasses, optimistically pining for Fall River of old and the halcyon days of their youth. Their nostalgic reminiscences served, perhaps, as an antidote for unfulfilled dreams and the oftentimes harsh realities of the "modern" world as they knew it; Fall River's cataclysmic economic decline, the Great Depression, and the horrors of two World Wars decidedly unpleasant topics.

Yet the vast majority of the papers produced have real substance, and at the core of each of them is the author's unmitigated passion for a particular subject. In many cases, the individuals who took pen to paper, or pecked away at typewriting machines, personally experienced the events of which they wrote, producing first-hand accounts with a narration little adulterated by the passage of time. Through personal reminiscences or those of their contemporaries, and with the aid of diaries, letters, and manuscripts then held in private collections, and now, perhaps lost, we are furnished with a glimpse of another age; the veil of time is lifted. Thus, the importance of these manuscripts cannot be understated; they are, indeed, compelling works, historical gems worthy of publication.

In some instances, the choice of words mimics the ideology and vernacular of the time, and may not be politically correct in the world of today; one must take into account the era in which they were written, and critique accordingly.

In addition to papers written in decades past, select contemporary works may also be included as part of the *Discourses on History* series.

In concluding an address he presented in 1937, Fall Riverite Thomas Richmond Burrell (1862-1953) uttered a statement that epitomizes the objective of the *Discourses on History* series:

> And if I in writing this imperfect paper, if you in listening patiently to its reading, if the Historical Society in placing it with its records, have lifted these names from the list of forgotten men, I feel with you, that we are well repaid.

Indeed, if the publication of these manuscripts brings this to pass, the efforts of these long dead recorders of history has been validated; if they have once again been given voice, the Fall River Historical Society has fully met its objective.

Michael Martins
Curator
Fall River Historical Society

1. Edward Stowe Adams.

About the Author

Edward Stowe Adams (1856-1948), was a lifelong resident of Fall River, Massachusetts. An original incorporator of the Fall River Historical Society, he was an extremely active member of the organization, serving as director and president, and was noted as the "dean of Fall River historians." Blessed at birth with an inquisitive mind, handsome features, and cultured, progressive parents, he was reared in an enlightened household; the strong moral convictions and civic and social responsibilities installed by his parents were mainstays throughout his long life.

His father, Robert Adams (1816-1900), was born in Ayr, Scotland, and immigrated to the United States with his parents as a child. He settled in Fall River in 1842 and established Adams Bookstore, a bookbindery, bookselling, and stationery business that was recognized as the most successful concern of its type in the city. Reams of paper and countless ledgers in myriad styles were needed to record the day-to-day business transitions of Fall River's lucrative textile mills, and numerous extant volumes of that nature bear the imprint of Adams Bookstore, a concern eagerly disposed to supply the demand. Throughout his lifetime, he was closely identified with the civic, political, and humanitarian affairs of his adopted city. A staunch abolitionist and active participant in the Underground Railroad in the decades prior to the Civil War, he habitually "conducted" fugitive slaves en route to freedom in Canada to safe houses in Massachusetts and Rhode Island. At the time of Robert Adams death, his obituary noted that "he made for himself an enviable record as a philanthropist. Not only did he give his money and moral influence toward the elevation of mankind, but a degree of hard personal effort was also contributed."

Edward's mother, née Lydia Ann Stowe (1823-1904), a native of Dedham, Massachusetts, was born into a progressive, well-educated family with ties to Fall River. She was a member of the first class of the Massachusetts State Normal School in Lexington and, as such, was one of the first professionally trained teachers in the United States; maintaining a lifelong interest in education, she was the first female member of the Fall River School Committee.

A devoted abolitionist, and early advocate for women's rights, she was an active participant in many charitable and educational affairs in Fall River, where she relocated after her marriage in 1844. She was a founding member of the Fall River Women's Union, an organization that assisted working women in various capacities, "regardless of race, religion, or class." Recognizing the necessity for the care of the elderly, particularly women, she and her husband donated a choice parcel of land on Highland Avenue upon which was constructed the Home for the Aged; opened in 1898, the organization still serves the needs of the elderly, and today operates as the Adams House in recognition of that family's longstanding support.

The Adams family welcomed many notable guests in their residence, providing young Edward the opportunity to become acquainted with many of the luminaries of the day, among them Frederick Douglass (c.1818-1895), who he remembered as "a personal friend of my father and … a man of commanding presence," and Sojourner Truth (c.1797-1883), who, he recalled, was "entertained for several days at our home." Of the latter he said she "sold her pictures at lectures saying, 'I sell the shadow to support the substance.'"

The erudite young man was educated privately during his formative years, graduated from the Fall River High School with the class of 1872, and was prepared for college at the West Newton English and Classical School in West Newton, Massachusetts. Entering Brown University, he was awarded a Bachelor of Philosophy in 1879.

His education complete, he returned to Fall River and entered his father's lucrative firm, from which he retired in 1917; additional business interests included investments in textile mills and banking concerns, on whose boards he served in various high-level capacities. Following the path laid by his parents, he became increasingly engaged in civic affairs and altruism, being considered a "leader in the city's educational and cultural progress," and "a cheerful, enthusiastic, and forceful worker for the public good." Raised in the Unitarian faith, he was an active member of his congregation, and served as church moderator for a number of years.

Well-travelled in the manner of the Grand Tour, he made numerous lengthy trips abroad, visiting the historical and cultural capitols of the world, in addition to more exotic, lesser-known locations. He married his first wife, née Eva J. Palmer (1856-1895), a native of Dover, New Hampshire, in Fall River on October 12, 1886; she died in 1895. Two years later, on July 29, 1897, he married, in Dedham, Massachusetts, Carrie Maria Smith (1855-1935), a native of that town. The second Mrs. Adams died in Fall River in 1935. Both unions were childless.

According to his friend and fellow historian, Arthur Sherman Phillips (1865-1941), Adams wrote "several important papers [*and*] articles ... all of which showed diligent research." Phillips further credited Adams with "render[*ing*] aid of great value [*and*] furnishing valuable information which has made several articles more accurate and complete" in his groundbreaking three-volume *Phillips History of Fall River*, published posthumously in 1944, 1945, and 1946.

Following Adams' death at the age of ninety-one on February 18, 1948, his obituary accurately noted that "his historical papers have served to perpetuate much important data pertaining to the city's background and progress which would otherwise have been lost to posterity."

It was a fitting epitaph to an extraordinary gentleman.

EDITORS' NOTE

On the evening of Monday, May, 23, 1938, Edward Stowe Adams presented his paper "Anti-Slavery Days in Fall River and the Operation of the Underground Railroad," illustrated with fifteen glass lantern slides, to the members of the Fall River Historical Society in the parish hall of the First Congregational Church; the presentation was extremely well received, later being presented in serial form in the *Fall River Herald News*.

Contained in this volume is an expanded version of Adam's original manuscript, which is housed in the Charlton Library of Fall River History at the Fall River Historical Society. The format of this manuscript has been slightly edited for punctuation and readability, with italicized information in square brackets added for the purposes of clarification and context. Illustrations include the fifteen original images selected by the author, supplemented with additional images pertinent to the text.

In order to preserve the integrity of the original manuscript, and in an attempt to retain the voice of the author, the phraseology and opinion conveyed in the text remain that of the writer, and do not reflect the views of the Fall River Historical Society.

1

ANTI-SLAVERY DAYS IN FALL RIVER
AND THE
OPERATION OF THE UNDERGROUND RAILROAD

Although the subject of this paper is Anti-Slavery and its results, I wish to give some earlier data pertaining to slavery.

Last November [*1937*], I had the pleasure of meeting Rudolf Frederick Haffenreffer (1902-1991) twice at his museum at Mount Hope [*King Philip Museum, Mount Hope Farm, Bristol, Rhode Island, later the Haffenreffer Museum of Anthropology, which became part of Brown University in 1955*]. His collection has been much enlarged since he invited the Fall River Historical Society to visit it in 1929. Although largely of Native American associations there is much pertaining to Bristol, Rhode Island, including valuable matter connected with Governor William Bradford (1729-1808), whose beautiful house is now Mr. Haffenreffer's summer home. In the course of the delightful conversation, Mr. Haffenreffer, having in some way learned of this proposed paper, said he had some early letters on the slave trade connected with Bristol which I might like to see and copy parts for this paper. I was pleased to avail myself of the opportunity, and his secretary, for another visit had selected some of the more interesting ones from and to James DeWolfe (1764-1837) of Bristol, who was known as the "Merchant King of Bristol," some of his fortune having been made in the slave trade. He is said to have entertained with a lavishness scarcely exceeded in the United States.

A 1796, letter from James DeWolfe to a man at St. Thomas, Virgin Islands: "15 slaves died after ship left St. Thomas—sold ship's cargo of 24,700 gallons," of what not mentioned but you can imagine.

From November to January, the ship *June* reported sales of "139 slaves from Africa."

Letter from Havana, Cuba, to James DeWolfe: "A few lots of slaves sold at $400 a head ready cash, time not far distant will be sold at $500 a head."

Another, letter, dated 1797 from Havana, Cuba: "prime negroes are selling at $400 to $500."

Another from St. Thomas, Virgin Islands: "have been boarded by the French and English examiners, but came out bright".

"There are very few Blackbirds here but 'purty' plenty at St. Croix."

Another: "seven negroes purchased for $800. Three sold for upwards of $900."

1805: "Bought six very fine fellows for $250 each."

Pertaining to Bristol, Rhode Island slave days, an 1807 letter from John DeWolfe (1760- 1841), to his brother, James: "I hear that slaves is risin and cannot be had under $300 a head."

Matanzas, Cuba, 1819: Alluded to coffee being properly packed, etc. also, "we can then buy 20 females much lower than now."

Earlier than above, in 1736: "7 choice cargoes of slaves $300 and $490," from Africa, were sold in Yorktown, Virginia.

Bristol is said to have followed Newport closely in the latter half of the century in the slave business. The slave trade in the District of Columbia was notorious; children from one year to eighteen months old were worth $100.

A History of the Town Freetown, Massachusetts [*by Palo Alto Pierce*] states that the slave trade was firmly established at the beginning of its history between New England and the West Indies. Slave auctions were held in the streets of some of the southern cities and mention is made of being held in the rotunda of a hotel in New Orleans.

Mr. Orrin Augustus Gardner (1867-1944) in his paper "Swansea: Its History and Story," given before the Fall River Historical Society on

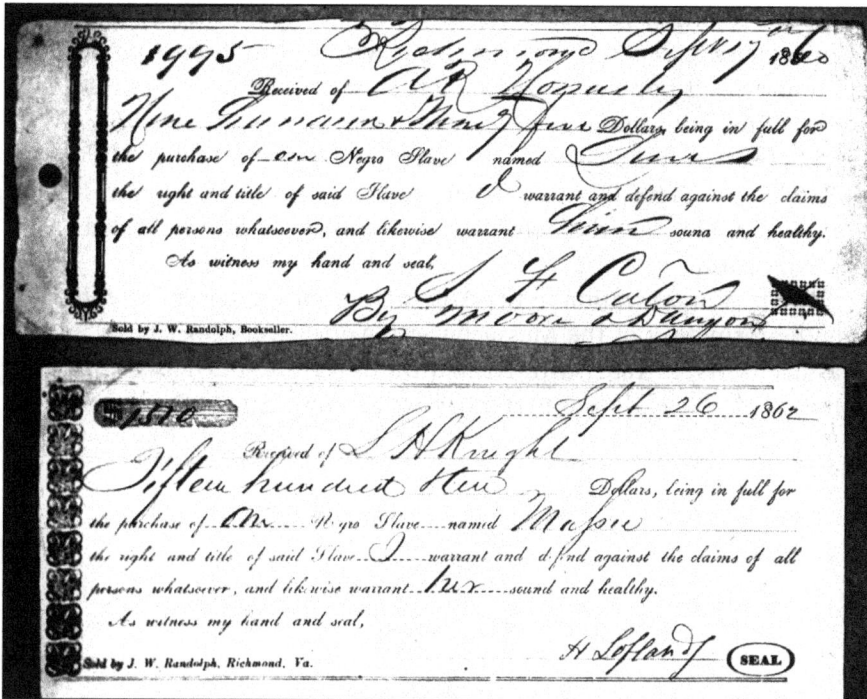

2. "Bills of Sale of slaves."

March 31, 1930, mentioned that a house built in that town by one of his early ancestors contained a huge dark room under the kitchen into which slaves were lowered through a trap door. Although slavery was abolished in Massachusetts in 1783, for twenty-five years after, slaves were mentioned in inventories with other goods and chattels, one was valued as high as £500, nearly $2,000, and were sometimes bequeathed in wills. Churches built in Colonial times had slave pews in parts of the galleries. The book, *Suckanasset: A History of Falmouth, Massachusetts 1661–1930 [by Theodate Geoffrey, nom de plume of Dorothy Wayman Godfrey (1893-1975)]* states that "the Quakers were given to taking up subscriptions to buy the freedom of negro and Indian slaves." A paper dated 1745 states: "Then received of Benjamin Gifford [1703-1788] forty shillings in Cash of ye old tenor towards freeing my negro boy Fortunates Sharpes by name, at the age of 25 years."

That the slave trade was a large and established business up to the time of the Civil War is shown from the following advertisements: a firm that established its main office in St. Louis, Missouri, had "cash for all negroes that might be offered"; an advertisement published in 1850 reads, "Willingness to separate husband from wife and mother from her little children to suit purchasers"; and another, published in St. Louis in 1855, states, "One thousand negroes wanted."

High prices were paid in 1859 and 1860: $1795.00 for a fellow forty years old, and $1100.00 to $1200.00 each for "three boys 10 years of age," and $1045.00 for "a girl of ten." The price of slaves often depended on the price of cotton.

The first organization in the Anti-slavery movement in New England was the formation of the Massachusetts Anti-Slavery Society in Boston, Massachusetts, in 1832, with Arnold Buffum (1782-1859) as its president —many of the early supporters were in New England, especially in

3. Arnold Buffum, 1826. "While a resident of Fall River became the first president of the Massachusetts Anti-Slavery Society."

Massachusetts and Rhode Island, among them, The Religious Society of Friends, or Quakers, as they were often called, who were distinguished for their liberal thought and kindly bearing as well as their simplicity of dress.

The Convention to Form a National Society met in Philadelphia, Pennsylvania, a year later, on December, 4-6, 1833. *The Declaration of Sentiments of the American Anti-Slavery Convention*, dated December 6, 1833, with an illustration, and printed on silk, 12 x 18 inches, are interesting:

ADOPTED AT THE FORMATION OF SAID SOCIETY, IN PHILADELPHIA, ON THE 4TH DAY OF DECEMBER 1833.

THE Convention, assembled in the city of Philadelphia, to organize a National Anti-Slavery Society, promptly seize the opportunity to promulgate the following DECLARATION OF SENTIMENTS, as cherished by them, in relation to the enslavement of one sixth portion of the American people.

More than fifty-seven years have elapsed since a band of patriots convened in this place to devise measures for the deliverance of this country from a foreign yoke. The corner-stone upon which they founded the TEMPLE OF FREEDOM was broadly this—"that all men are created equal; that they are endowed by their Creator with certain inalienable rights; that among these are life, LIBERTY, and the pursuit of happiness." At the sound of their trumpet-call, three millions of people rose up as from the sleep of death, and rushed to the strife of blood; deeming it more glorious to die instantly as freemen, than desirable to live one hour as slaves. They were few in number—poor in resources; but the honest conviction that TRUTH, JUSTICE, and RIGHT were on their side, made them invincible.

We have met together for the achievement of an enterprise without which that of our fathers is incomplete, and which, for its magnitude, solemnity, and probable results upon the destiny of the world, as far transcends theirs as moral truth does physical force.

In purity of motive, in earnestness of zeal, in decision of purpose, in intrepidity of action, in steadfastness of faith, in sincerity of spirit, we would not be inferior to them.

Their principles led them to wage war against their oppressors, and to spill human blood like water, in order to be free. *Ours* forbid the doing of evil that good may come, and lead us to reject, and to entreat the oppressed to reject, the use of all carnal weapons for deliverance from bondage; relying solely upon those which are spiritual and mighty through God to the pulling down of strongholds.

Their measures were physical resistance—the marshaling in arms—the hostile array—the mortal encounter. *Ours* shall be such only as the opposition of moral purity to moral corruption—the destruction of error by the potency of truth— the overthrow of prejudice by the power of love—and the abolition of slavery by the spirit of repentance.

Their grievances, great as they were, were trifling in comparison with the wrongs and sufferings of those for whom we plead. Our fathers were never slaves—never bought and sold like cattle— never shut out from the light of knowledge and religion—never subjected to the lash of brutal taskmasters.

But those for whose emancipation we are striving— constituting, at the present time, at least one sixth part of our countrymen—are recognized by the law, and treated by their fellow-beings, as marketable commodities, as goods and chattels, as brute beasts; are plundered daily of the fruits of their toil, without redress—really enjoying no constitutional nor legal protection from licentious and murderous outrages upon their persons; are ruthlessly torn asunder—the tender babe from the arms of its frantic mother—the heart-broken wife from her weeping husband—at the caprice or pleasure of irresponsible tyrants. For the crime of having a dark complexion, they suffer the pangs of hunger, the infliction of stripes, and the ignominy of brutal servitude. They are kept in heathenish darkness by laws expressly enacted to make their instruction a criminal offense.

These are the prominent circumstances in the condition of more than two millions of our people, the proof of which may be found in thousands of indisputable facts, and in the laws of the slaveholding States.

Hence we maintain, that in view of the civil and religious

privileges of this nation, the guilt of its oppression is unequaled by any other on the face of the earth; and, therefore,

That it is bound to repent instantly, to undo the heavy burdens, to break every yoke, and to let the oppressed go free.

We further maintain, that no man has a right to enslave or imbrute his brother—to hold or acknowledge him, for one moment, as a piece of merchandise—to keep back his hire by fraud—or to brutalize his mind by denying him the means of intellectual, social, and moral improvement.

We fully and unanimously recognize the sovereignty of each State to legislate exclusively on the subject of the slavery which is tolerated within its limits; we concede that Congress, *under the present national compact*, has no right to interfere with any of the Slave States in relation to this momentous subject.

But we maintain that Congress has a right, and is solemnly bound, to suppress the domestic slave-trade between the several States, and to abolish slavery in those portions of our territory which the Constitution has placed under its exclusive jurisdiction.

These are our views and principles—these our designs and measures. With entire confidence in the overruling justice of God, we plant ourselves upon the Declaration of our Independence and the truths of Divine Revelation, as upon the Everlasting Rock.

We shall organize Anti-Slavery Societies, if possible, in every city, town, and village in our land.

We shall send forth agents to lift up the voice of remonstrance, of warning, of entreaty, and rebuke.

We shall circulate, unsparingly and extensively, anti-slavery tracts and periodicals.

We shall enlist the pulpit and the press in the cause of the suffering and the dumb.

We shall aim at a purification of the churches from all participation in the guilt of slavery.

We shall encourage the labor of freemen rather than that of slaves, by giving a preference to their productions; and

We shall spare no exertions nor means to bring the whole nation to speedy repentance.

Our trust for victory is solely in God. *We* may be personally defeated, but our principles, never. TRUTH, JUSTICE, REASON, HUMANITY, must and will gloriously triumph.

Submitting this DECLARATION to the candid examination of the people of this country, and of the friends of liberty throughout the world, we hereby affix our signatures to it; pledging ourselves that, under the guidance and by the help of Almighty God, we will do all that in us lies, consistently with this Declaration of our principles, to overthrow the most execrable system of slavery that has ever been witnessed upon earth—to deliver our land from its deadliest curse—to wipe out the foulest stain which rests upon our national escutcheon— and to secure to the colored population of the United States all the rights and privileges which belong to them as men and as Americans—come what may to our persons, our interests, or our reputation—whether we live to witness the triumph of LIBERTY, JUSTICE, and HUMANITY, or perish untimely as martyrs in this great, benevolent, and holy cause.

Since this paper was started a book has been published entitled *Two Quaker Sisters,* written from the original diaries of Mrs. William Buffington Chace, née Elizabeth Buffum (1806-1899), and her sister, Mrs. Reverend Nehemiah Gorham Lovell, née Lucy Buffum (1829-1882), with an introduction by Malcolm Read Lovell (1889-1975), formerly of Fall River, the son of the late William Buffum Lovell (1847-1925). There is much of interest pertaining to early Anti-Slavery matters, as the two sisters mentioned, also their sister Sarah Gould Buffum (1805-1834), who married Nathaniel Briggs Borden (1801-1865), were daughters of Arnold Buffum, who lived in Fall River until moving to Valley Falls, Rhode Island, in 1839. While in Fall River he aided in establishing a private school for young children. Later, he was known as the "Quaker Hatter" from manufacturing hats in which he introduced many improvements, but his

4. Masthead from William Lloyd Garrison's abolitionist newspaper, *The Liberator*.

life work was in the freedom of the slaves, lecturing here and abroad. I will quote from the book later.

The history of the Anti-Slavery movement whether connected with Fall River, or Boston, or New England, would be incomplete without the work of William Lloyd Garrison (1805-1879), who began lecturing for the cause in 1830 and started *The Liberator* in 1831, a weekly paper devoted to Anti-Slavery that continued until 1865.

A meeting [*of the Boston Female Anti-Slavery Society held*] in Boston on October 21, 1835, was broken up and "Garrison was placed in jail overnight to save him from the violence of a respectable mob which sought to destroy him for preaching the dangerous doctrine that all men are created equal."

William Lloyd Garrison spoke in Fall River a number of times—his energy and perseverance both in lecturing and in *The Liberator* accomplished much. His vigorous attitude is best shown in his own words in the first issue of the paper: "I am in earnest, I will not equivocate, I will not excuse, I will not retreat a single inch, and I will be heard."

In July, 1834, a meeting attended by one-thousand persons was held in the First Baptist Meeting House, to consider forming an Anti-Slavery Society in Fall River. "Two reports were read, the majority favorable to forming, and the other unfavorable but favored eliciting information on the subject." There was some disturbance but no damage done of any importance being prevented by early adjournment.

The following month, in August, 1834, a meeting adopted a Constitution, stating: "We believe that Slavery as existing in the United States is a crying sin," and that, "This Society shall be called the Fall River Anti-Slavery Society—object, the Abolition of Slavery."

Long communications on Anti-Slavery with editorials on the same were frequently published in *The Fall River Monitor*. The following year a Female Anti-Slavery Society was formed in Fall River, about 1835, of twenty-seven members, whose names are given in the book, *Two Quaker Sisters*. The same year an editorial in a Fall River newspaper stated: "To hold slaves is a right guaranteed to the South by the Constitution." The intense feeling then existing is shown in the following letter:

Fall River, April 9th, 1835

Mr. Nathaniel B[*riggs*] Borden,
         Sir:

        The request, which, 'by the direction of the Fall River Anti Slavery Society' you have made for the use of the house of the Unitarian Society for the purpose of a meeting to hear a lecture from the Reverend Mr. [*Samuel Joseph*] May [*1797-1871*] on the subject of Slavery on some evening between Saturday and Wednesday next" has been before the undersigned members of the Committee of the Unitarian Society and has been considered with every disposition to grant the request, provided they could feel satisfied that the proposed meeting could be held without danger or injury to the property of the Society—But the high degree of excitement of the public mind upon the subject of Slavery, which was shown on the occasion of the last public meeting upon this subject that is known to us to have been held here, seems to us to demand that we should not, assume the responsibility of complying with the request, especially as we have not been able to see or consult with the other member of the Committee.

With entire respect we are very respectfully your obt. servts.

H[*ezekiah*] Battelle [*1790-1872*]

        Committee of the U[*nitarian*] S[*ociety*]

Wm. H[*enry*] Hawkins [*1805-1878*]

N.B. We should have delayed longer our reply in order to have seen Mr. Holder Borden [*1798-1837*], the other member of our Committee, had we not believed that the Anti-Slavery Society would be very desirous of an early answer.

5. William Henry Hawkins.

Within ten years of this, meetings were held in this church [*First Congregational Church*], also in the Episcopal Church Pearl Street Chapel, and Fireman's Hall in Fall River. In 1839, at a meeting of the Bristol County Anti-Slavery Society in Fall River, a resolution offered to establish a paper as the organ of the Society called forth a warm debate.

The annual meeting of the Fall River Anti-Slavery Society in July, held at First Baptist Meeting House, was addressed by Arnold Buffum. The Fall River Female Anti-Slavery Society held its meeting same day—the Buffums, and Lovells were prominent officers.

Fairs for the benefit of the cause were often held. In 1840 appeared a long appeal for articles for an Anti-Slavery fair in Boston. In 1841, Abraham Bowen (1803-1889) reported in the *Fall River All Sorts and Tiverton Advertiser* of $300 received from an Anti-Slavery Fair saying, "Fall River people are not slow in doing the handsome thing in aid of a good cause."

December 7, 1844, in *The Fall River Monitor*: "Fall River Anti-Slavery Sewing Circle deem it expedient to hold a fair to procure lectures, etc. in behalf of the oppressed countrymen," it was signed by seven ladies:

Sarah J. Sexton

Mrs. Edward Buffinton neé Sarah Ann Hathaway (1816-1882)

Sarah D. Harris (1816-1889)

Susan (Garfield) Beers (c.1813-1873), the widow of Charles Beers, later Mrs. John V. Hall

Mrs. Robert Adams, née Lydia Ann Stowe (1823-1904)

Hannah T. Almy (1823-1898), later Mrs. Thomas Almy

Sarah Congdon Wilbur (1827-1856), later Mrs. Hon. Dr. Robert Thompson Davis

The following year a fair was held at Berean Temple, which was located at the corner of Second and Borden Streets, on the site of Columbian Hall, which was destroyed in the "Great Fire of 1843."

March 17, 1855, in *The Fall River Monitor*: "A very successful fair was held by Ladies of Fall River Anti-Fugitive Slave Law Society"—a card of thanks appeared.

6. "View of the Great Fire in Fall River, July 2, 1843."

7. "View of Fall River Looking South Down Main Street," 1839.

The Fall River Anti-Slavery Society, in 1838, had 112 members, and the Female Anti-Slavery Society had 106. Both Societies held their annual meetings that year in the Baptist Meeting House; the Fall River Temperance Society held its meeting in the Methodist Chapel.

A Tennessee newspaper on the Pro-Slavery controversy regarding Henry Clay (1777-1852), and Martin Van Buren (1782-1862), said: "Turning loose the unbridled fanaticism of the Abolitionists upon an institution by which the South has resolved to stand until the last drop of blood shall gurgle from their veins." The southern attitude is illustrated in the following notice of a sale of eight slaves, names given, "to satisfy a mortgage in favor of the directors of the Theological Seminary of the Synod of South Carolina and Georgia."

The Fall River Monitor endorsed the Whigs. Its editorials were often bitter and terms used, amusing. Loco-Focoism and Slavery: "Every week furnishes new evidence that the Loco Focos of the North are becoming more and more united with the views of the South upon the subject of slavery. [*The Locofoco Party was a radical wing of the Democratic Party, organized in New York in 1835.*]

On September 22, 1838, a newspaper column was devoted to the report of a committee of the managers of the Fall River Anti-Slavery Society

8. Mrs. William Buffington Chace, née Elizabeth Buffum.

on the objects of political action. A November 10th editorial, headed "Friends of the Slaves," stated: "Choose ye whom ye will have to serve you. Whether Mr. N[athaniel] B[riggs] Borden, who is one of the first and foremost abolitionists in the state, or Mr. [Henry] Williams [1805-1887], who supports [Martin] Van Buren in his opposition to Abolitionists." Nathaniel B. Borden was defeated.

Candidates for political office in Fall River were sometimes questioned as to their views on slavery. Letters appeared in the press endorsing men for state offices who were friends of the slaves.

In October, 1839, Nathaniel B. Borden wrote to His Excellency Edward Everett (1794-1865), who was a candidate for reelection as Governor asking two questions:

> 1st. Are you in favor of the immediate abolition of slavery in the District of Columbia and of the slave traffic between the states of the Union?
>
> 2nd. Are you opposed to the admission into the Union of any new state, the constitution of which tolerates domestic slavery?

Mr. Everett replied to both questions in the affirmative; his original letter is in existence.

The prejudices and bitterness toward prominent abolitionists are depicted in *Two Quaker Sisters*, the Anti-Slavery Reminiscences of Elizabeth (Buffum) Chace, while living in Fall River before removing to Valley Falls, Rhode Island, in 1839, from which I will quote at length—first published in 1891:

> We went to our Yearly Meeting at Newport, [Rhode Island] and there slavery was the chief topic of conversation, at the hotel where many Friends were staying; so stirred were people everywhere, either for or against the system, by the new awakening. But almost everybody was against us. They denounced *The Liberator*; [William Lloyd] Garrison was an infidel; slavery could only be cut off gradually; the colored race must be colonized in Africa. There was a general treatment of such as were known to be abolitionists, as suspicious persons – persons to be overlooked and avoided.

The bitterness mentioned by Mrs. Chace in Newport is perhaps explained in the following statement by a writer on early Rhode Island:

"The most important factor in Newport commerce for fully half a century was the African slave trade." [*William Babcock Weeden (1834-1912)* Early Rhode Island: A Social History of the People].

The same author, after "speaking of the doings of the rough privateers," wrote, "But what shall we say of the pious and most respectable 'elder' of Newport, who sent slavers with uniform success from Newport? On the Sunday after arrival, he always returned thanks 'that an overruling Providence had been pleased to bring to this land of freedom another cargo of benighted heathen to enjoy the blessing of a Gospel dispensation.'"

Quoting further from Mrs. Chace's *Anti-Slavery Reminiscences*:

> At that time the prejudice against color, throughout New England, was even stronger than the pro-slavery spirit. On one occasion, my husband [*William Buffington Chace (1800-1870)*] and I went to Boston, to attend the annual meeting of the New England Anti-Slavery Society. Accompanied by a gentleman we drove to Taunton [*Massachusetts*] from Fall River, there to take the railroad, which at that time furnished only one car for the journey. As we entered the car, Samuel Rodman [*1792-1876*], an Anti-Slavery leader from New Bedford and a highly respectable, well-dressed colored man and his wife, from the same town, also took seats therein. The conductor came and ordered the colored people to leave the car. We all remonstrated, of course, but without avail. He called the superintendent, who peremptorily repeated the order. The colored people got out quietly, and we did the same, but not so quietly, and retired to the waiting-room, leaving the car empty. The officials held a conference outside, and the conductor soon informed us that an extra car had been put on for the negroes, and invited us to take the seats we had left. We held a little conference among ourselves, and then every one of us entered the car with the colored people. The superintendent was very angry, but he did not quite dare to order us out, so he assured us that our conduct would avail nothing, for no negroes would ever be permitted to be mixed up with white people on that road. They were mixed up with us, however, on that day, and we found them intelligent, agreeable companions.
>
> In some cases, persons who were opposed to slavery and were willing to work for abolition, nevertheless strongly objected to any association with colored persons in their Anti-Slavery labors. After removal to Valley Falls, [*Rhode Island*], our Anti-Slavery attitude soon put us under the ban of disapproval among our Providence, [*Rhode Island*] friends.

The Underground Railroad was the name popularly applied before the Civil War to the system of aiding fugitive slaves to escape from their masters and elude pursuit.

Prof. Wilbur Henry Siebert (1866-1961) of Ohio State University, in 1898 wrote a book with this title of several hundred pages [*The Underground Railroad from Slavery to Freedom*] in which he says:

> By furnishing food and shelter as well as advice to fugitives, northern abolitionists enabled thousands of slaves to escape to Canada, beyond the read of the Fugitive Slave Law. Houses along the routes were known as stations, those who directly assisted the fugitives were known as conductors, and those who made contributions of money, clothing, etc. were known as stockholders in the enterprise.

Many of those concerned in the service were fined heavily for violating the Fugitive Slave Law but occasional punishments did not deter the ardent abolitionists.

The station most frequently alluded to in Fall River was the home of Nathaniel B. Borden on the east side of Second Street opposite the Borden Block [*demolished in the 1930s*]. The present home of the Fall River Historical Society, when in its original location, was another station of the Underground Railroad. Regarding which our President, Oliver Snow Hawes (1860-1938) gives the following, including some early items of interest:

> When the Historical Society's building stood on its original site, 28 Columbia Street, from 1843 to 1869, [*Friend*] William Hill [*1799-1881*] occupied it as owner a portion of that time. He bought it from the bankrupt estate of Andrew Robeson [*Jr. (1817-1874)*] in the late [*18*]40s or early [*18*]50s. [*In fact, Hill purchased the property from Thomas T. Lea, on July 7, 1854 for the sum of $13,825; Lea purchased the property from Robeson on July 15, 1849.*] Mr. Hill was a well-to-do Quaker of North Berwick, Maine, and had a <u>positively</u> uncanny scent for bargains, near and far. He was a partner here in the [*18*]50s of Nathan Buffinton (1790-1865) in the spool thread business, and married, as his first wife, my mother's aunt, Elizabeth [*née Buffum (1802-1859)*] of Maine. My mother, [*Mrs. William Mowry Hawes, née*] Louisa Buffum [*1838-1912*] of North Berwick, Maine, came here to teach school in 1855 and lived with the Hill family on Columbia Street for two years in the big stone 'Robeson House.'

9. "The home of Nathaniel B. Borden on the east side of Second Street ... was an important station of the Underground Railroad." The structure, at 40 Second Street, was razed in the 1930s.

All she ever told me about the house was its elegance and the false book-case, which concealed a closet and a trap door in the floor covering a staircase into a closed room in the cellar. This room was used as a wine cellar by Mr. Robeson originally, and later in his time as a refuge for runaway slaves who arriving at New Bedford were being passed through Fall River to Providence by night on their way to Canada, if possible. That any slaves were there in my mother's time, I do not know positively, but that was always my childish impression, and as Friend Hill was an outstanding member of The [*Religious*] Society of Friends, I see no reason for doubting it now. He would certainly have been willing to help at all times, if emergency aid was needed, and his wife was a most tender hearted lady beloved by all who knew her, an early and very strong abolitionist.

The false bookcase, now in the Fall River Historical Society's collection, containing supposed sets of books in fine leather bindings are interesting

10. Friend William Hill.

deceptions being only blocks of wood fastened together, the titles on the edges include: *British Poets*; *Egyptian Antiquities*; *Travels in Tartary*; and others. One title was *Chips from an Old Block*; was this suggested from the essay of Charles Lamb (1775-1834), *Books which are no Books*? Somewhat similar arrangements are mentioned elsewhere, sometimes only boxes on the shelves back of which the whole is released by a spring. [*The leather-bound spines of the false books on the door, tooled in gilt, bear the imprint of "R & J. Adams" the bookseller and bookbindery business of Fall River abolitionist Robert Adams and his brother, John Adams.*]

The William Barnabas Canedy (1784-1855) home at 2634 North Main Street, Fall River, this side of Steep Brook, harbored runaway slaves. Miss Flora E. Mosher (1867-1947) wrote [*in her paper "The Toll House and the East End," presented before the Fall River Historical Society on October 20, 1933*] of a young colored man calling at her father, Isaac N. Mosher's

11. Louisa Buffum, later Mrs. William Mowry Hawes, circa 1857, when she resided with her uncle, Friend William Hill, in the stone mansion on Columbia Street.

(1841-1915) home in Lakeville, Massachusetts, asking for food and shelter for the night on his way to Canada.

Historically the Underground Railroad is of continued interest as about three years ago in 1935, Prof. Wilbur Henry Siebert, already alluded to, gave a paper on this subject before that outstanding organization the American Antiquarian Society in Worcester, Massachusetts, entitled *The Underground Railroad in Massachusetts*, which was published in pamphlet form of over seventy pages, with a map of the routes.

The first chapter is entitled "Underground Railroad Routes from New Bedford, Fall River, and Eastern Connecticut." After mentioning the arrival of fugitives on Cape Cod thence to New Bedford, he states, "The regular Underground route extended from New Bedford to Fall River—this town had been since the 1830s an important center for forwarding the runaways."

12. The "stone mansion" built for Andrew Robeson, Jr. at 28 Columbia Street, Fall River, Massachusetts, in an aerial view photographed during the residency of Friend William Hill. The mansion was used as a station on the Underground Railroad by the Robeson and Hill families.

13. William Barnabas Canedy residence, "South of Steep Brook," now 2634 North Main Street, Fall River, Massachusetts; the residence was a station on the Underground Railroad.

Quoting again from *Anti-Slavery Reminiscences* by Elizabeth (Buffum) Chace, after removing to Valley Falls, Rhode Island, which give a vivid account of the connections in this vicinity:

> From the time of the arrival of [*fugitive slave*] James Curry [*born c.1815*] at Fall River, and his departure for Canada, in 1839, that town became an important station on the so-called underground railroad. Slaves in Virginia would secure passage, either secretly or with the consent of the captains, in small trading vessels, at Norfolk or Portsmouth, and thus

14. Residence of Mr. & Mrs. William Buffington Chace, Valley Falls, Rhode Island, an active station on the Underground Railroad.

be brought into some port in New England, where their fate depended on the circumstances into which they happened to fall. A few, landing at some towns on Cape Cod, would reach New Bedford, and thence be sent by an abolitionist there to Fall River, to be sheltered by Nathaniel B. Borden and his wife, who was my sister Sarah [*Gould Buffum*], and sent by them to my home at Valley Falls, in the darkness of the night, and in a closed carriage, with Robert Adams [*1816-1900*], a most faithful Friend, as their conductor. Here, we received them, and after preparing them for the journey, my husband would accompany them a short distance, on the Providence and Worcester Railroad, acquaint the conductor with the facts, enlist his interest in their behalf, and then leave them in his care. They were then transferred at Worcester to the Vermont road, from which, by a previous general arrangement, they were received by a Unitarian clergyman named Young, and sent by him to Canada, where they uniformly arrived safely.

This clergyman was Reverend Joshua Young (1823-1904), later settled in Fall River [*as pastor at the Unitarian Church, 1868 to 1875. Rev. Young officiated at the funeral of abolitionist John Brown (1800-1859), at North Elba, New York, on December 8, 1859. For Rev. Young's recollections of "The Funeral of John Brown," see Supplement, page 87.*]

One evening, in answer to a summons at our door, we were met by Mr. [*Robert*] Adams and a person, apparently in a woman's Quaker costume, whose face was concealed by a thick veil. The person, however, proved to be a large, noble-looking colored man, whose story was soon told. He had escaped from Virginia, bringing away with him a wife and child. Reaching New Bedford, he had found employment, which he had quietly pursued for eleven months. [*He was*] a very valuable piece of property (I think he was a blacksmith); his master had spared no pains in discovering his whereabouts and finally traced him to New Bedford. Coming to Boston, he secured the services of a constable, and repaired to New Bedford, and went prowling round in search of his victim. But the colored people of that town, discovering the purpose of the searchers, communicated with some of the few abolitionists, and the man was hurried off to Fall River, before the man-stealer had time to find him; and my sister Sarah and her husband Nathaniel [*B.*] Borden dressed him in Quaker bonnet and shawl, and sent him off in the daylight, not daring to keep him till night, lest his master should follow immediately.

His master, after searching for him a whole day in New Bedford, had returned to Boston, very much disgusted with the indifference of the 'Yankee Mudsills,' as the lordly Southerners used to call New Englanders, to the misfortunes of the slave-holders.

Another time we were aroused about midnight, by the arrival of the good Friend [*Robert*] Adams, with two young men, about twenty-four years old. They also were from Portsmouth, Virginia. They had each secured passage on a small trading vessel, bound for Wareham, [*Massachusetts*], through the friendly interest of the colored steward, but without the knowledge of each other, or of the Captain and crew of the vessel; and they were strangers to one another before their escape. The steward concealed one in the hold, and the other in his own berth, in the little cabin he had all to himself, and he carried them food in the night.

15. Robert Adams, "the so-called conductor of the Underground Railroad who took fugitive slaves ... to Valley Falls or Pawtucket [*Rhode Island*] in the darkness of the night."

Another night, good Robert Adams aroused us with a carriage full—a woman, and three children. She had escaped from Maryland some time before, with her family, and established herself at Fall River as a laundress; had made herself a home, and was doing well. Her eldest boy, of seventeen years, worked in a stable; and after a while, had gone six miles away to work for a farmer. Soon after this, the same officer who arrested [*fugitive slave*] Anthony Burns [*1834-1862*], in Boston, arrived in Fall River, and was seen prowling around the neighborhood where colored people lived; and especially and suspiciously, peering into the stable, where this woman's son had previously worked.

We kept them three or four days, in hourly fear and expectation of the arrival of the slave-catcher; our doors and windows fastened by day as well as by night, not daring to let our neighbors know who were our guests, lest someone should betray them. We told our children*, all at that time under fourteen years of age, of the fine of one thousand dollars, and the imprisonment of six months that awaited us, in case the officer should come, and we should refuse to give these poor people up; and they heroically planned how, in such an event, they would take care of everything; and especially, that they would be good, and do just as we wished, during our absence.

[*Samuel Buffington Chace and Elizabeth (Buffum) Chace were the parents of: George Arnold Chace (1830-1839); Adelia Bartlett Chace (1832-1839); Susan Elizabeth Chace (1834-1837); John Gould Chace (1837-1842); Oliver Chace (1841-1843); Samuel Oliver Chace (1843-1867); Arnold Buffum Chace (1845-1932); Elizabeth Buffum "Lillie" Chace (Mrs. John Crawford Wyman 1847-1929); Edward Gould Chace (1849-1871) and Mary Elizabeth Chace (Mrs. Horace Rundlett Chaney, later Mrs. James Pike Tolman 1852-1928).]*

Miss Annie Malcolm Slade (1878-1963) of Yonkers, New York, a granddaughter of Albion King Slade (1823-1909) and Mary Bridge (Canedy) Slade (1826-1882) has written that slaves were hidden in the cellar of the double house where they lived, on 335-337 Pine Street [*in Fall River*]. Quoting her own words: "The sheriff came to investigate but Mrs. Slade received him as a social caller and talked so industriously about everything but slavery that she got him out of the house without his remembering what he came for."

16. Anthony Burns' arrest and trial under the Fugitive Slave Law resulted in heated protest and rioting by abolitionists in Boston, Massachusetts, in 1854.

17. *Above:* Albion King Slade.

18. *Left:* Mrs. Albion King Slade, née Mary Bridge Canedy. As an abolitionist, she had the ability to remain composed in tense situations. Two of her sisters, Betsey Leonard Candey, and Anne Chaloner Graves Canedy, went south to teach the freedmen.

An "Address of the Ladies Anti-Slavery Society of Fall River to the Christian Women of Fall River" was published in pamphlet form about 1840, which began as follows:

> Dear sisters—Impelled by a deep sense of our own duty, and a strong desire to awaken you to a more thorough conviction of yours, we venture to address you on a subject of the most vital importance to your country, to yourselves, to your children. We doubt not that most of you are acquainted with the fact, that there are in our country, 2,500,000 men, women and children, who, for no crime of theirs, are held as property, are driven to labor, for which they receive no wages; that they are sold as marketable commodities. The Ladies Anti-Slavery Society of Fall River, hold public meetings, monthly, where they read Anti-Slavery publications, and speak often one to another of these things.

This was signed by eleven ladies—the officers and executive committee.

One of the Resolutions adopted at a meeting of the abolitionists held in the Town House [*located at Town Avenue, north of Central Street*], Fall River, on Friday Evening, June 30, 1843:

> Resolved, that instead of taking part in the celebration of the ensuing Fourth of July, we will form a procession and wear a badge of mourning, preceded by a muffled drum, expressive of our sympathy in behalf of the slave population of this country, and follow the procession of the day. Persons wishing to join the procession will please leave their names with the committee of arrangements.

The committee was made up of the following:

Richard Cornell French (1805–1851)
Mrs. Nathaniel Briggs Borden, née Sarah Gould Buffum (1805–1854)
Robert Adams (1816–1900)
Catharine C. Crank (born c.1827, later Mrs. Elisha Simpson)
Stephen Leonard French (1803–1885)
Mrs. James T. Lindsey, née Abby Jane Terry (1812–1860)
J. G. Fuller
Abraham Bowen (1803–1889)

19. Mrs. Reverend Nehemiah Gorham Lovell, née Lucy Buffum.

[*The extent to which some ladies of the Fall River Female Anti-Slavery Society were willing to go in the Anti-Slavery cause was clearly conditional, and on at least one occasion caused great consternation, as is evidenced in a statement made by Elizabeth (Buffum) Chace in* Two Quaker Sisters, *that was not mentioned in Adam's original paper: "In the village of Fall River were a few very respectable young colored women, who came to our meetings. One evening, soon after the Society was formed, my sister Lucy* [Buffum Lovell] *and I went to see these negro women and invited them to join. This raised such a storm among some of the leading members, that for a time, it threatened the dissolution of the Society. They said they had no objection to the women attending the meetings, and they were willing to help and encourage them in every way, but they did not think it was at all proper to invite them to join the Society, thus putting them on an equality with ourselves. Lucy and I maintained our ground, however, and the colored women were admitted."*

Two of the "young colored women" referred to may have been among the members of the committee that organized the July 4ᵗʰ, 1843 procession, referenced previously: In the 1850 United States Federal Census, *under the column headed "Color," Catharine C. (Crank) Simpson, a Massachusetts native, is identified as "Mulatto"; her husband, Elisha Simpson, a Connecticut native, is listed as "Black." In that same 1850 document, Abby Jane (Terry) Lindsey, a Massachusetts native, is identified as "Black," and in 1860, she is listed as "Mulatto"; her husband, James T. Lindsey, a North Carolina native, is identified in a corresponding manner.*

The planned procession, however, likely never took place: On July 2, 1843, the center of Fall River was destroyed in a conflagration, referred to as the "Great Fire of 1843."]

The last name listed was that of Abraham Bowen, a strong abolitionist who cared for runaway slaves in his house at 175 Rock Street opposite the Episcopal Church [*Church of the Ascension*]. He published a small newspaper called *The Fall River All Sorts and Tiverton Advertiser*, which contained many bright and pointed items.

Quoting from the *March of Democracy: A History of the United States* by James Truslow Adams (1878-1949): "The intensity of the situation was shown in the Congress of 1849 when five of the leading questions involved slavery, one being publicly selling slaves in the District of Columbia."

20. Abraham Bowen residence, 43 (now 175) Rock Street, Fall River, Massachusetts. The house was a station on the Underground Railroad.

"At this time [*Daniel*] Webster [*1782-1852*] made his famous Seventh of March speech [*March 7, 1850, in the Unites States Senate*], which exasperated the anti-slavery elements in the north where sentiment had been extremely bitter against the laws for the capture and return of slaves who had escaped from their masters into Free States."

Frequent and lengthy communications from individuals appeared in *The Fall River Monitor*. From one are a few lines:

Annual Meeting of the Fall River Anti-Slavery Society

N[*athaniel*] B. Borden elected President, Reverend Asa Bronson [*1798-1866*], Vice-President. The exercises were truly interesting, performances of the choir unusually effective and interesting. The address of Mr. [*William Lloyd*] Garrison [*1805-1879*] gave general satisfaction to a numerous and highly respectable audience—he has awakened a new interest in behalf of the Anti-Slavery cause. Fall River is true Anti-Slavery

21. Nathaniel Briggs Borden, "one of Fall River's early outstanding men interested in all humanitiarin matters and a strong abolitionist."

22. Reverend Asa Bronson.

> ground. Twelve Resolutions were adopted, among them 'That the war against slavery is a moral conflict....'

The editor, however, made only a slight allusion to the above meeting but also stated: "In the evening the Female Anti-Slavery Society held a meeting in the First Baptist Meeting House but as we were not present at either of these two meetings we were unable to speak from personal knowledge of the lecture and addresses."

Squire James Ford (1774-1873) was the editor of *The Fall River Monitor*, the only newspaper then regularly published in Fall River—from this comment and others later, it is evident that Squire Ford as he was frequently spoken of, was not in hearty sympathy with the Anti-Slavery movement. Quoting from another editorial, he said: "Limits of the paper prevent publishing all communications—some of which are trash," then says, "Slavery is a curse and we shall be glad to see it abolished but never will it be effected while some of the above opinions are promulgated."

"It is admitted that they cannot be liberated without the master's consent. Is it possible that any man can expect to conciliate the slave holders by calling them man stealers, murderers and robbers? This would be strange reasoning on any subject."

23. James Ford, "lawyer, postmaster, and vigerous editor of *The Fall River Monitor*."

Under the Fugitive Slave Act of 1850, the ownership of a fugitive slave was determined by the simple affidavit of the person claiming the slave. The testimony of the alleged fugitive could not be received in evidence.

Reverend Orin Fowler (1791-1852), pastor of the First Congregational Church of this city, was elected a member of the Massachusetts Senate in 1847, and the following year, November, 1848, was elected a member of Congress from the Fall River district. In 1850, *The Fall River Monitor* expressed "admiration at the course of Hon. Mr. Fowler in the national legislature in acting and voting on the side of freedom and voted against the Fugitive Slave Bill in Congress." Squire James Ford had evidently begun to modify his views. Two weeks later, on September 21, 1850, high praise was given Reverend Fowler in an editorial in *The Fall River Monitor,* and the Whig organ of New England saying "that there is not a district in the U[*nited*] S[*tates*] more faithfully represented than ours."

A little later a lengthy editorial in *The Fall River Monitor* took exception to the *Boston Advertiser* quoting rather bitterly from the *Fall River News* regarding Mr. Fowler—nearly three columns including letters on the subject were published and the controversy continued. Later, the Whigs of Fall River adopted resolutions highly commendatory of Reverend Fowler's efforts to secure the principles of Liberty and Justice. Among many petitions presented by Reverend Fowler in Congress for repeal of the Fugitive Slave Law was one of Dr. Jason Hawes Archer (1794-1864) and 202 others from Fall River.

The meetings in Fall River of the Anti-Fugitive Slave Law Society, Free Soil Convention, and Whig Convention—all adopted resolutions against the Fugitive Slave Law and committees of leading citizens were appointed in each.

24. Reverend Orin Fowler, "Pastor of the First Congressional Church [*and*] author of the first history of Fall River. He spoke not only from the pulpit ... as a member of Congress his voice was heard in behalf of the oppressed, as were those of many of his fellow citizens in that great humanitarin movement for the freedom of the slaves."

During the months following, there certainly must have been lively times here as disclosed in the vigorous controversies between *The Fall River Monitor* and the *Fall River News* on the nomination of Reverend Fowler. "Loco-focos" and "Loco thunder" were terms frequently used—this was a term applied to ultra-radicals. Reverend Fowler was re-elected in 1850.

In 1850, *The Fall River Monitor* published a long editorial on dissolution of the Union and slavery. Soon after, the same paper said, "We have never been able to see the necessity or propriety of whites and blacks blending together in the public schools."

The same year the Ladies Anti-Slavery Society held a tea party at the Town Hall [*and Market Building*] in aid of fugitive slaves. Anti-Slavery sentiment often became a strong factor in the political situation even here in Fall River. In 1851, Nathaniel B. Borden declined to be a Whig candidate for state representative —in a communication he stated, "I regard the Fugitive Slave Law as among the wickedest of modern legislation."

When the election of Charles Sumner (1811-1874) as senator was pending before the Massachusetts Legislature, Mr. Borden, being a member, asked for instructions from home as to how he should vote—Sumner was elected by one vote and Mr. Borden was credited with the election of Charles Sumner. *The Newport Herald* said, "Yes, and that act should stamp him with everlasting disgrace." Two years later, in November, 1853, Charles Sumner spoke here in Fall River in Town Hall [*and Market Building*] on the great question, "Are you for Freedom or are you for Slavery?"

The Hutchinson Family Singers, became identified with the Anti-Slavery and Temperance movements, and made a successful tour of New England in 1841. Soon after, they appeared in New York City and achieved an immediate success—later they travelled in Great Britain, creating great interest. [*The Hutchinson Family Singers were an American singing group with a repertoire that included songs on abolitionist, temperance, and women's rights themes. The group included: Jesse Hutchinson (1813-1853); Adoniram Judson Hutchinson (1817-1859); John Wallace Hutchinson (1821-1908); Asa Burnham Hutchinson (1823-1884); and Abby Jermima Hutchinson (1829-1892), later Mrs. Ludlow Patton.*]

They were co-workers with [*William Lloyd*] Garrison and other abolitionists, and sang a number of times in Fall River in connection with the anti-slavery movement. Even the Editor of *The Fall River Monitor*, after one of their concerts here in 1850, said: "Their singing is natural, national, simple and vibrates on the heart of humanity. We hope they will call this way again."

25. The Hutchinson Family Singers, 1843.

The Hutchinson family sang before President Abraham Lincoln (1809-1865) in the White House, and in 1862 were granted a permit to pass within the lines of the Army of the Potomac and to sing to the soldiers. A book of the words of some of their songs [*The Hutchinson Family's Book of Words*] was published in 1851.

The following is an Emancipation Song entitled "Get Off the Track," with words composed and adapted to a slave melody, advocating the emancipation of the slaves, and illustrating the onward progress of the Anti-Slavery cause in the United States.

GET OFF THE TRACK!

Ho! The car emancipation,
Rides majestic through our nation,
Bearing on its train the story,
Liberty! A nation's glory.
Roll it along! roll it along!
Roll it along! through the nation,
Freedom's car, Emancipation.

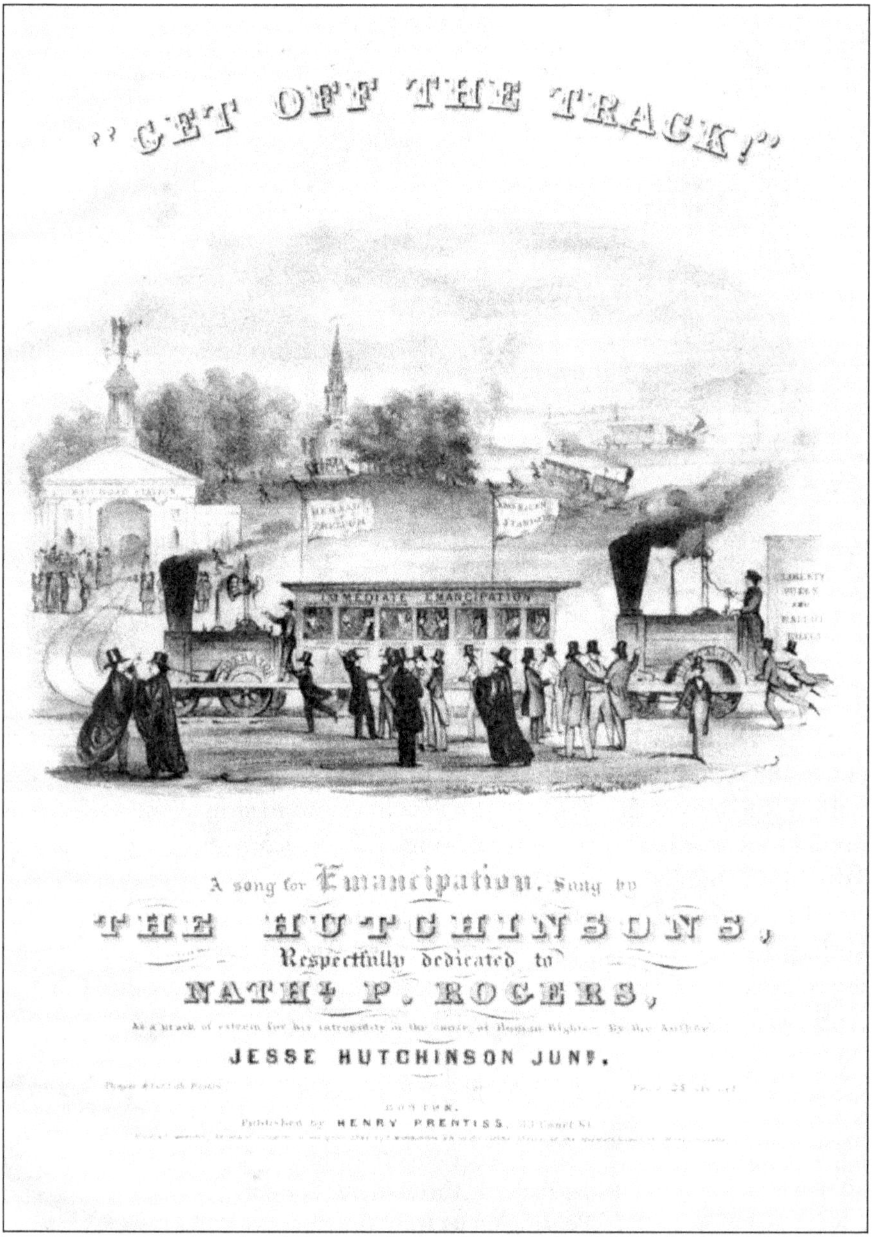

26. "Get Off the Track!" sheet music, 1844.

Men of various predilections,
Frightened, run in all directions,
Merchants, Editors, Physicians,
Lawyers, priests, and politicians,
Get out of the way! every station,
Clear the track, Emancipation.

Let the ministers and churches
Leave behind sectarian lurches,
Jump on board the car of freedom,
Ere it be too late to need them.
Sound the alarm! pulpits thunder,
Ere too late to see your blunder.

All true friends of emancipation,
Haste to freedom's railway station,
Quick into the cars get seated;
All is ready and completed.
"Put on the steam! all are crying,
While the liberty flags are flying.

Hear the mighty car wheels humming;
Now look out! the engine's coming!
Church-and-statesmen, hear the thunder,
Clear the track, or you'll fall under.
Get off the track! all are singing
While the "Liberty Bell" is ringing.

On, triumphant, see them bearing,
Through sectarian rubbish tearing;
The bell, and whistle, and the steaming,
Startle thousands from their dreaming.
Look out for the cars! while the bell rings,
Ere the sound your funeral knell rings.

See the people run to meet us!
At the stations thousands greet us;
All take seats with exultation,
In the car, Emancipation.
Huzza! Huzza! Emancipation,
Soon will bless our happy nation.

The humanitarian sentiment was continually stirred by the Massachu-
setts group of authors, John Greenleaf Whittier (1807-1892), James Russell
Lowell (1819-1891), Ralph Waldo Emerson (1803-1882), Henry Wadsworth
Longfellow (1807-1882), and others.

In 1852 appeared Harriet Beecher Stowe's [*Mrs. Calvin Ellis Stowe,
née Harriet Elisabeth Beecher (1811-1896)*] book *Uncle Tom's Cabin*. James
Truslow Adams (1878-1949), the historian, says: "It aroused such a storm
of emotion and anger as had no other book in the annals of America and
probably in the world"—300,000 copies were sold in the first year and it
was translated into twenty foreign languages. Rufus Choate (1799-1859)
is quoted as saying that "Uncle Tom's Cabin would make 2,000,000
Abolitionists."

A February, 1854, letter from Andrew Robeson, Jr. to Nathaniel B.
Borden regarding an escaped slave:

New Bedford, Feby. 18th 1854

Nathaniel B. Borden

My dear Sir:

You may recollect the circumstances that took place a few
weeks since, the attempt to capture a slave, who escaped to this
place in a vessel from Norfolk, Va., they came at that time very
near capturing him. We have just now got information that his
owner has offered a high reward for him and that they have
actually formed all their plans to take him without delay. We
think it imprudent for him to be here after the boat arrives and
I could not think of any better plan than sending him to Fall
River, if you can keep him out of sight for a short time. We shall
be obliged to send him to Canada, as his owner is very much
provoked, I presume at what has been said in the papers. We
are collecting some money to help him on the way, and if we
don't get enough just now we will do more when I see you.

Very truly,

Andrew Robeson

Quote regarding a citizens meeting in 1854:

Notice having been received that a reprobate judge had
decided to yield to the demands of slavery and send back
Anthony Burns to the land of whips and chains, Doctors

27. "An illustration from Harriet Beecher Stowe's *Uncle Tom's Cabin*, published in 1852."

28. Andrew Robeson, Jr.

29. Dr. Foster Hooper.

30. Dr. James Mott Aldrich.

31. Hon. Dr. Robert Thompson Davis.

[*Foster*] Hooper [*1805-1870*], [*James Mott*] Aldrich [*1817-1896*], [*Isaac*] Fiske [*1791-1873*], and [*Hon. Robert Thompson*] Davis [*1823-1906*]—N[*athaniel*] B. Borden, [*Louis*] Lapham [*1810-1881*], [*Josiah Coleman*] Blaisdell [*1820-1900*], [*Reverend John*] Westall [*1816-1890*], and others, adopted strong resolutions urging the repeal of the Fugitive Slave Law."

The eight names read were all very prominent men in Fall River.

Although the Anti-Slavery spirit grew and prospered … the bitterness continued to some extent at the North. Ministers differed on the subject and quoted from the Bible pro and con in support of their views. Families and outstanding citizens also differed. That the First Baptist Church in Fall River was opposed to slavery was shown not only by the frequent Anti-Slavery meetings held there, but also from their records. The First Baptist Church prior to 1855 adopted the following resolution regarding Anti-Slavery: "No circumstances justify holding slaves. We will not invite or allow a slave holding minister to occupy the pulpit or invite or allow a slave holder to commune with us as a church."

Abraham Lincoln, while Senator in 1858, made his famous speech: "A house divided against itself cannot stand—I believe this government cannot endure permanently half slave and half free."

When John Brown (1800-1859), the radical abolitionist, seized the National Arsenal at Harper's Ferry, Virginia, hoping thereby to establish a defensible station for fugitive slaves, was hung on December 2, 1859, my father's [*Robert Adams*] sympathy was aroused and he draped his store [*Robert Adams, Bookseller and Stationer, 29 South Main Street*] window in mourning—Dr. Phineas Washington Leland (1798-1873), a very prominent citizen of Fall River and the Customs Collector of the district walked into the store and said to my father, "You should share the same fate."

It seems to have been truly said that, "Within eighteen months of that event, many a northern regiment, as it marched to the seat of war, sang that which will always remain the war song of the great conflict the [*John Brown Song*]:

John Brown Song

John Brown's Body lies a mouldering in the grave,
John Brown's Body lies a mouldering in the grave,
John Brown's Body lies a mouldering in the grave.
But his soul goes marching on!

32. John Brown, abolitionist, an engraving after an 1859 photograph.

CHORUS:
Glory, glory, hallelujah!
Glory, glory, hallelujah!
Glory, glory, hallelujah!
His soul goes marching on!

He's gone to be a soldier in the Army of the Lord,
He's gone to be a soldier in the Army of the Lord,
He's gone to be a soldier in the Army of the Lord.
His soul's marching on!

CHORUS:
Glory, glory, hallelujah!
Glory, glory, hallelujah!
Glory, glory, hallelujah!
His soul goes marching on!

John Brown's knapsack is strapped upon his back,
John Brown's knapsack is strapped upon his back,
John Brown's knapsack is strapped upon his back.
His soul goes marching on!

CHORUS:
Glory, glory, hallelujah!
Glory, glory, hallelujah!
Glory, glory, hallelujah!
His soul goes marching on!

John Brown died that the slaves might be free.
John Brown died that the slaves might be free.
John Brown died that the slaves might be free.
His soul goes marching on!

CHORUS:
Glory, glory, hallelujah!
Glory, glory, hallelujah!
Glory, glory, hallelujah!
His soul goes marching on!

Departing for a moment from our subject may I say that Dr. Phineas W. Leland wrote a poem of twenty verses entitled "Fall River As It Was and As It Is," first published in the first number of a small paper in 1847 called the *Tea Party Gazette*, also in the second edition of *The Fall River Directory* in 1855:

P. W. Leland,

33. Dr. Phineas Washington Leland, "although opposed to Anti-Slavery and called a 'copperhead' [*he*] was a man of literary testes—president of the Fall River Athenaeum and Collector of Customs of the Fall River District."

Still rolls the *Titequit* along,
Where gathered once the warrior throng
Of *Metacomet* stern:
Where moose, and dear, and panther stole
Through forest wild and sedgy pool,
And fields of odorous fern.

Here at our feet the *Quequechan*,
Unaltered by the art of man,
Leap't headlong o'er the Fall:
No dam across its bed then lay,
The foaming, dashing flood to stay;
Nature was all in all.

Above, the out-stretched *Wahtahpee*,
Beneath, the swelling, heaving sea,
Each in their beauty lie:
Nor quay, nor pier, nor vessel bound,
Nor stately mill, nor pleasure ground,
Responded to the eye.

But one vast forest met the gaze,
A tangled wild or thorny maze,
Untouched by skillful hand;
Where lived and dreamed the red man wild,
Lord of the realm on which he smiled;
Sole owner of the land!

And here with beasts had dwelt his race
Unnumbered ages: made the chase
His pastime and his toil;
Or warring with his brother wild,
Who, like himself, a forest child,
Dwelt on some border soil.

'Tis said the *Dane*, in days of yore,
Had in his wanderings reached this shore,
And called Mount Hope, *Montaup*;
And men well versed in things of old,
Believe the story dimly told—
Cut in the "Dighton Rock."

Strange people they, those Danes confessed,
Their card to leave on stones impressed,
Millions unborn to teach.
That here had stayed the white man bold,
In quest of Empire or of gold,
Beyond the old world's reach.

Long ages past—forgot the Dane,
When lo! The Pilgrim hither came,
Trusting in God alone;
His was the mission to endure,
Privation—Hunger,—to secure
An Empire all his own.

The Indian fled, or passed away,
Like dew-drop in the blush of day,
No more to wander free,
Where countless ages roamed his race,
Free as the air of upper space,
Strange—strange his destiny!

O'er the new realm Art waved her wand,
Old forests vanished, and the land
Teamed with a busy throng;
And on the hill and in the vale.
Was heard the saw, the axe and flail,
The merry shout and song.

Paths roads became, and soon a mill
Moved by the wind, stood on some hill,
The wonder of the place:
Here rose a church—a cabin there,
Here fields of corn fenced in with care—
Anon, an open space.

Beside that church, where lofty trees
Waved proudly in the summer's breeze.
Or bent beneath the storm,
The school-house stood—a structure rude,
Of logs unhewn, and joinings crude,
Clay-patched and rough, but warm.

And here were taught a hardy race
Their rights to know, their foes to face,
Should such invade their soil:
Men of, and for their age were they,
Of iron nerve and bold essay—
Made strong by healthful toil.

But changed is all : Our fathers sleep
In lonely graves beside the deep,
Beneath the living host:
Where hamlet once, and late a ville,
And smiling City crowns the hill—
"WE'LL TRY," its only boast.

Dams now the dashing falls control.
Wheels locked in wheels revolving roll,
And forge, and saw, and stone
Obey the liquid impulse strong.
As onward leaps the flood along—
A triumph nobly won.

And, magic like, the cotton mill,
In beauty decks the swelling hill,
Spanning the chasm broad:
On centres neatly balanced list
Ten thousand spindles formed to twist
The silky, fibrous cord,

Here seething metal takes new forms,
Is rolled or cast, and so adorns
The parlor or the mill;
Or drawn in wire, or plates, or rails,
For screws or hoops, or bolts or nails—
A grand display of skill.

Our Printers, too, with art divine,
On rollers etch their chaste design—
A rose, or vine, or plaid;
Then o'er these run the fabric white,
When suddenly is brought to sight
The pattern skill had made.

And here, but erst, but whitened sails
Light breezes courted, and in gales
Battled with billows mad,
Steam now, the wind and tide defies,
And through the ocean proudly hies
The DREAM that FULTON had.

And onward still our course we run,
New fields to win, as we have won
Rich trophies of the past:
Be ours the labor here to plant
A city that shall all enchant
Whose lot may here be cast.

Mrs. Dr. Howard Perry Bellows, formerly Miss Mary Anna Clarke (1851-1946), now [in 1938] living in Cambridge, Massachusetts, the daughter of Dr. John Lewis Clarke (1812-1880) who resided here in Fall River on the north east corner of North Main and Cherry Streets, after 1854, has furnished some interesting data. Her grandfather Dr. Peleg Clarke (1784-1875) of Richmond, Rhode Island, organized the first Anti-Slavery Society in Rhode Island and was connected with the Underground Railroad.

Mrs. Bellows recalled, in later years her father, pointing to some cane seated chairs, said: "Mary Anna thee ought to have great respect for those chairs for [William Lloyd] Garrison, Wendell Phillips [1811-1884] and all those men used to sit in them," and further said that these two names, and also: Reverend Parker Pillsbury (1809-1898); Charles Calistus Burleigh (1811-1878); Frederick Douglass (c.1818-1895), the Grimké Sisters [Sarah Moore Grimké (1792-1873) and Angelina Emily Grimké (1805-1879)]; Harriet Beecher Stowe, and others were household words.

Mrs. Harry Theodore Harding, née Anna Robinson Fiske (1845-1929), daughter of Dr. Isaac Fiske, who lived in the house at 263 Pine Street [in Fall River], told [her cousin] Mrs. Dr. Howard P. Bellows, then Miss Mary Anna Clarke, it was "not safe to go into the attic, for there might be a runaway slave up there."

A cousin of Mrs. Dr. Bellows, Dr. Henry Bradford Clarke (1827-1888), an abolitionist in New Bedford, had a cook [Isabella White] who had been a slave, and was sent north packed in a piano box, but en route the box was placed the wrong end head down for twenty-four hours but the occupant survived.

34. Town Hall and Market Building, circa mid-19th century. The building was the scene of numerous Anti-Slavery meetings and charitable affairs for that cause.

[Isabella White was born in Stafford County, Virginia, in 1837, and is consistently listed as "Mulatto" in the United States Federal Census; *by 1860, she was residing in New Bedford, Massachusetts. The widow of Solomon White, she was the mother of two children: Solomon White, Jr., born in New York circa 1858; and Maria White, born in Massachusetts circa 1859. In order to maintain a position as a live-in domestic, she boarded her children with George F. Fletcher, a laborer, and his wife Margaret; the couple were African American natives of Washington, D.C.*

By 1860 she was employed as a domestic by Dr. Daniel Wilder (1811-1888), a homeopathic physician, and his wife, née Mary Ann Goss (1815-1902). According to their granddaughter, the Wilders were "actively interested in the abolition of slavery and were in Faneuil Hall in Boston the night that William Lloyd Garrison was dragged out and through the streets by a mob, October 21, 1835. Grandpa and Grandma escaped from the mob by going behind that stage where they had been seated with other abolitionist sympathizers and into an alley behind the hall."

By 1865, Isabella had entered the employment of homeopathic physician Dr. Henry B. Clarke and his wife, née Martha C. Little (1836-1914); both were ardently sympathetic to the abolitionist cause.

35. William Mowry Hawes captioned this photograph: "Members of the Young Men's Republican Club of Fall River, Massachusetts. Organized by the Free Soiler's or Anti-Slavery men who ran John Charles Freemont for President in 1856 on the first Republican Party ticket. They were defeated by the Democrats under James Buchanan but gained a glorious victory with Abraham Lincoln in 1860. the rest is history. This photograph was taken in 1857 or 1858." The group was also known as the "Wide Awakes."

The men were members of families with strong abolitionist sympathies. *Standing, left to right:* James H. Olney; George Robinson Fiske; Benjamin Buffinton. *Seated, left to right:* Thomas A. Slade; Charles Jarvis Holmes; William Mowry Hawes; Joseph Abraham Bowen.

According to the 1880 United States Federal Census, Isabella was residing at 68 Union Street and "keeping house" for her son, a "shoe master" and her daughter, a "domestic." She died in New Bedford on February 6, 1924.]

Mrs. Dr. Bellows said it was a sad day when as a little girl she heard the bells tolling at the time John Brown was hung, on December 2, 1859 —soon after her father brought in a quantity of handbills saying, "A job for thee, little girl"—there was to be an Anti-Slavery meeting, and posters were to be put up all over the city headed, "John Brown Hung," but tops were to be cut off, as her "father did not think the heading polite."

Mrs. Dr. Bellows mentioned a children's fair in the old Music Hall for the freedmen that raised $500, "and we scraped lint out of school hours while our elders were busy knitting, and sewing, and having fairs." She, mentioned her cousin, George Robinson Fiske (1837-1918), a member of the "Wide Awakes"—an organization of young Republicans active in the campaign for Abraham Lincoln, who wore white enamel cloth capes. She

36. Reverend Peter Britton Haughwout.

also sent copies of long letters from William Lloyd Garrison paying tribute to her grandfather, and from Frederick Douglass after her father's death. She also wrote that Reverend John Westall, a prominent man of Fall River and an intimate friend of her family, addressed every company of soldiers leaving here at the time of the Civil War.

On April 21, 1861, Reverend Peter Britton Haughwout (1828-1877) delivered in the First Baptist Church, "An Address Suggested by the Times," which made such an impression that eight very prominent citizens of various denominations, speaking of it as a "highly patriotic discourse," asked the next day for a copy for immediate publication and it was forthwith printed.

The Civil War was largely the outcome of the Anti-Slavery movement, but it brought many and serious problems, especially resulting from the Emancipation Proclamation in 1863, but those who had labored in the Anti-Slavery cause continued their interest and assistance in many ways to the former slaves who were thrown on their own resources, not only then but for some years after.

This is shown in the letters of the three Fall River ladies from which extracts are given. Also in cooperation with The Freedmen's Bureau, established in 1865 in the United States War Department with refugees, freedmen, and abandoned lands among its objects; provisions, fuel, and clothing were to be distributed free of charge to destitute freedmen and refugees.

Eunice Hathaway (Congdon) Dixon, (1821-1907)

Eunice Hathaway Congdon, [later Mrs. George Emerson Dixon] was the first person from Fall River of whom I have any knowledge, to teach and aid the African Americans, at the south. She was a native of New Bedford, became a teacher in Fall River in the one room schoolhouse corner of North Main and Prospect Streets, resigned about 1853 and went south, interested in the education of the colored people, several years before the Civil War. She had many trying experiences both before and during the Civil War. Her courage, loyalty, and profound interest in her chosen work was unbounded.

Permit me to say that while a teacher in Fall River, Miss Congdon became a very intimate friend of several ladies, including my mother, [Mrs. Robert Adams, née Lydia Ann Stowe]. Her annual visits north in the summer and continued correspondence furnished much information pertaining to her experiences at the south—of these she later wrote

37. Company F, 26th Regiment Massachusetts Volunteer Infantry, assembled on North Main Street, April 5, 1864, while on furlough from New Orleans, Louisiana.

38. Eunice Hathaway (Congdon) Dixon, "a teacher in Fall River [*and*] a devoted worker in the south before, during, and long after the Civil War. A pupil, in a long tribute to her memory said, 'Before school hours in the morning, and after school hours in the afternoon, this earnest woman labored in the poor homes of the freedmen.'"

interesting reminiscences which friends at Hampton University tried to have published. The manuscripts later disappeared, but some letters prior to 1865 have been saved, which told of her difficulties encountered in obtaining permits to pass through the military lines during the Civil War and the early conditions of the slaves.

In 1864, she went to Yorktown, Virginia, under the auspices of the Friends Association in Philadelphia, stating, "I am anxious to see schools established in Richmond and elsewhere, not only for the freedmen but free public schools for the whites. When I first came here there was but one teacher, now a year later there are 16."

Writing of Williamsburg, Virginia: "One of the most aristocratic and oldest towns on the peninsula—most of the white people there, are secessionists and only kept in subjection by union soldiers and they treated the teachers with great contempt at first," but later seemed glad to send their children to school. Quoting a sentence, "These Southerners will get some very wholesome ideas from the (so called) 'Greasy Yankees'." Speaking of the great loss of President Lincoln, she says the freedmen speak of him as their Liberator and Moses, who has led them out of Egypt.

> Some of the people here when forced to believe the terrible news of his death gave up entirely. Now that the paroled rebel soldiers are returning they (the negroes) are timid about being out after dark lest some violence be done them.
>
> Quite a number of soldiers have returned near us and act in a threatening defiant manner toward the colored people.
>
> My school is still large, have had 475 different scholars in day school besides a great many different ones in my class in night school and sewing and knitting schools.
>
> This is a work that pays—I never engaged in anything which afforded me so much real satisfaction and can see the fruits of my labors.
>
> One girl who walks seven miles to school to me every morning brought me the most beautiful roses I ever saw.

The African American race was emotional and religiously inclined—quite a volume of their spiritual songs was published a number of years ago.

39. Mrs. Robert Adams, née Lydia Ann Stowe. According to the author, "Miss Congdon became a very intimate friend of several ladies, including my mother."

Mrs. George E. Dixon [*née Eunice Hathaway Congdon*] transcribed for me "Uncle Pete's Counsel to the Newly Married," consisting of three pages interesting in dialect and thought, a few lines of which I will read.

Uncle Pete's Counsel to the Newly Married

My chil'ren, lub one anoder, b'ar wid one anoder, be faithful ter one anoder. You habe started on a long journey, many rough places am in de road, many trubbles will spring up by de wayside; but go on hand an' hand togedder; lub one anoder, an' no matter what comes onter you, you will be happy for lub will sweeten every sorrer, lighten every load, make de sun shine in eban de bery cloudiest wedder. I knows it will, my chil'ren, 'case I'se been ober de groun'. Ole Aggy an' I hab trabbled de road. Hand in hand we hab gone ober de rocks, fru de mud, in de hot burning sand; been out togedder in de bold, an' de rain, an' de storm, fur nigh onter forty yar, but we hab clung to one anodder; an' fru ebery ting in de bery darkest days, de sun ob joy an' peace hab broke fru de clouds, an' sent him bressed rays inter our hearts. We started jess like two young saplin's you's seed agrowin' side by side in de woods.

Explanation of the term "contraband," from *Southern Workman*, May 1906:

Six weeks after the fall of Fort Sumter [*April 13, 1861*] General Benjamin F[*ranklin*] Butler [*1818-1893*] took command of the Union army in eastern Virginia—the next day three Negro men [*Frank Baker, Shepard Mallory, and James Townsend*] were brought before him who had fled from the Confederate fortifications to escape their masters purpose to take them further south.

The next morning General Butler responded to a flag of truce request for return of Colonel [*Charles King*] Mallory's [*1820-1875*] property, being the three men.

Butler issued his famous declaration that as all property used for warfare is contraband, to be taken and held by a contestant whenever possible, that as slaves were being used as property against the United States, fugitives would not be returned into slavery by its army, but would be regarded as contrabands of war, this did much toward the solution of the slave question and is said to have prepared the way for the Emancipation Proclamation.

The magical word "contraband" thrilled the north and south and the word spread rapidly among the people, and thousands flocked into the Union lines and the United States had a new problem. Abandoned plantation buildings were put to use—tents and shanties erected—some rations were issued by the government. Day and night schools were soon opened for the contrabands—teachers were sent down by the American Missionary Society [*from the Congregational and Presbyterian churches*] and The Religious Society of Friends. The year 1863 transformed the contrabands into freedmen, and General Butler ordered a large schoolhouse built at Hampton, Virginia, early in 1864, and known as the Butler Contraband School, in which Miss Congdon taught. A little later General Samuel Chapman Armstrong (1839-1893) started the educational work which became Hampton Normal & Agricultural Institute [*later called Hampton Institute, now Hampton University.*]

In 1873, General Armstrong secured for General Butler the superintendence of Mr. and Mrs. George E. Dixon—one wing of the Butler school building being made into a dwelling for the Dixons. Mrs. Dixon [*née Eunice Hathaway Congdon*] was principal of the school for two years, her first report gave the number of pupils 194, ages from 5 to 24 years. She then formed a preparatory department in the Normal School.

The next letter was from Danville, which is on the border line of Virginia and North Carolina, and expresses great pleasure at the prospect of a box of clothing so greatly needed.

> The school room is not comfortably warm, have secured two old government stoves that are being patched up. We have a government house secured, (an old barrack of a hospital) and am having it fitted up for school and church—to aid in this, I have made an appeal to Sarah [*R.*] Jones [*born c.1832*] of Fall River, (I may say Miss Jones kept a private school in the Quaker Meeting House on Franklin Street, North West corner of High Street) to get the Central [*Congregational*], Stone, and Baptist Churches to take up a contribution for the benefit of the '1st African Church in Danville.' I am determined to raise the money in some way. Our committee in Philadelphia is going to appeal to the Secretary of War to give the building.

"Our association has been very remiss in furnishing us with means so we have absolutely suffered for the necessary comforts," and speaks of lack of bedding for themselves. "I shall be glad when the soldiers go from here for they are so demoralized themselves that they demoralize the freedmen."

In Danville in 1866, a colored boy named Edmund either attended Miss Congdon's school or made her acquaintance—he had run away several times from a very cruel master, been caught, hung up by his thumbs and lashed on the back until the blood ran. Miss Congdon arranged for him to run away again and she would bring him north on her summer vacation—she secreted him on the train between the seats covering him with the large skirts of those days and baggage—before the train started his master walked through the train swearing vengeance but did not find him. Edmund was left in Philadelphia, Pennsylvania, but soon after came to Fall River, my father, Robert Adams, having arranged to take him, and he lived in our family a number of years and attended school. He was thoroughly honest and hardworking but not very successful, and continued through forty years working more or less for our family.

[*Edmund E. Turner, the son of William and Matilda (Hoge) Turner, was a native of Danville, Virginia, born circa 1849; he was consistently listed in the* United States Federal Census *as "Black." By 1870, he was residing in Fall River, and for a brief period was "working on* [a] *steamboat." Shortly thereafter, he began his long association with the Adams family, employed as a servant, and, by 1880, as their coachman. According to the* Fall River City Directory, *he spent several years as a "laborer" and "teamster" before spending the remainder of his working life as a gardener for the Adams family at their residence at 660 Rock Street.*

His first wife, née Annie M. Seeley (1851-1905), was a native of Orange County, New York. The couple were married in 1870, and were the parents of five children: Frederick A. Turner (1870-1889); Edward Willard Turner (1872-1932); Mary Ella Turner (1875-1971), the wife of Elmer Ten Thompson; Charles Norman Turner (1879-1960); and Gertrude L. Turner (1882-1938). The latter married three times: William Bass, Frederick Volter, and Frederick Potter.

Illiterate at the time of his arrival in Fall River, he was able to read and write within a decade, perhaps encouraged by his wife, who was literate, and the Adams family, who placed a strong emphasis on education; all of the Turner children were educated.

40. Eunice Hathaway (Congdon) Dixon captioned this photograph: "Edmund Commander <u>before</u> your boxes came," referring to "the change due to boxes of clothing received from [*abolitionists*] from Fall River."

41. Eunice Hathaway (Congdon) Dixon captioned this photograph: "Edmund Commander <u>after</u> your boxes came," referring to "the change due to boxes of clothing received from [*abolitionists*] from Fall River."

42. Quaker Meeting House, Fall River, Massachusetts.

Edmund married his second wife, Ella L. (Johnson) Davis Melton, a Georgia native, in Fall River on June 15, 1905. He died at his Fall River residence on May 29, 1920.]

Viney [*A.*] Fields was another whom Miss Congdon brought north, and lived in the family of Oliver Buffinton (1805-1885), and his wife, née Elizabeth Mason Reynolds (1805-1892), and later built a home. [*A native of Virginia, born circa 1847, Viney A. Fields, who was unmarried, was consistently identified as "Black" in the* United States Federal Census; *she was employed by Oliver Buffinton and his wife, and, later, by their son, Francis Buffinton (1846-1916), until circa 1910, after which she was employed as a "Laundress for private families." She last appears in the 1920 edition of the* Fall River City Directory, *residing at 370 Linden Street where she had made her home for several years.*]

Among others Miss Congdon brought north was Mary Oliver. [*A native of Virginia, born circa 1845, Mary Oliver was identified as "Mulatto," in the* 1865 Massachusetts State Census; *she was a domestic employed in Fall River by Joseph Ferdinand Lindsey (1802-1885)*].

The Quakers in England were much interested in the colored schools in the United States, and a Friends organization sent a man, George Emerson Dixon (1826-1885) by name, to visit these schools with a view of giving some assistance. Among various schools visited, he stopped one night in Danville at the house occupied by the white teachers—about midnight Miss Congdon was awakened by someone attempting to open the window in her room—she called "George" and the marauders retired, not having thought of there being a man in the house. It was currently reported on the street next day that it was the intention "to kill the nigger teachers."

Later Miss Congdon and George E. Dixon were married [*in Guilford, North Carolina, on September 26, 1866*] but they continued the work hoping as she wrote that: "Unitedly we may be a means of doing much good to these poor benighted children." They built a small home on the grounds at Hampton Institute. Through Mr. Dixon's influence she wrote that much has been and is being done in England for the relief of the suffering here where there are schools under his superintendence. The boxes of clothing from Fall River are always spoken of in all letters with much appreciation.

Later Mr. and Mrs. Dixon went to England, and travelled and lectured on the American Freedmen and their great needs, and solicited funds to be used in the education of African American young men and women as teachers of their people. The sum of $10,000 was thus raised and appropriated to Hampton Institute for the benefit of fifty or sixty young men and women from Virginia and North Carolina, largely former pupils of Mrs. Dixon.

Booker Taliaferro Washington (1856-1915) was at one time a pupil of Miss Congdon, and later became principal of Tuskegee Institute [*now Tuskegee University, which he founded in 1881*]. Time will not permit of speaking of her continued interest and connection with Hampton, where she spent her last years, nor reading the splendid tribute to her memory by a former student in 1907.

Having spoken of the African American race as spiritual and emotional —many were also keen with bright and original remarks, I hear a colored maid, on seeing the whitish appearance of water coming from the faucet , say, "De fog has got into the water." Squire James Ford enjoyed telling this anecdote: a colored couple went to his office to be married, after they were united the man stepped to Squire Ford, touching him on the shoulder, and said, "Massa, you charge this?"

Betsey Leonard Canedy, (1816-1898)

Betsey Leonard Canedy of the well-known large family on North Main Street, this side of Steep Brook, after teaching in Fall River several years, resigned in the early 1860s, having been appointed by the New England Freedman's Aid Society, a teacher of Freed People in Norfolk, Virginia, and later, at Newbern, North Carolina. [*Her father and mother, William Barnabas Canedy (1784-1855) and his wife, née Susan Hughes Luther (1778-1858), were the parents of thirteen children, hence the "large family" reference.*]

Her sister, Anne Chaloner Graves Canedy (1821-1866), also resigned as a teacher in Fall River about the same time to teach at the south. Both of these ladies wrote interesting letters to friends in Fall River, of their work and experiences from which I will quote.

Newbern, North Carolina, was captured by General Ambrose Burnside (1824-1881) in 1862. Miss Betsey Canedy wrote that "it was the first rebel city in North Carolina where a Free School for Freedmen was established." Soon after her arrival she had 350 registered, with 320 present at one time, stating, "We are crowded with earnest, anxious pupils. I taught 145 yesterday without assistance—there is work for ten teachers instead of five." She also said, "I am perfectly well and unreservedly glad that I am here."

From a letter dated February, 1864:

> Through you allow me to thank your circle in behalf of my 200 and many more of their destitute kith and kin for contents of two of the most judiciously filled boxes that I have ever seen opened in the department. I am delighted and surprised that you should have found so many willing hearts and able hands to enter upon this unpopular work. I wish you could see the transforming influence that an exchange of rags for decent clothing has upon these poor creatures—they had to leave everything behind them when the rebels were approaching.

She wrote from Norfolk, Virginia, in 1865: "The freed people were told when the schools were opened here that all the Yankee teachers wanted was 'to get a church full of the children together and give them chloroform and then pack them and send them north and sell them'—but something taught them better."

She also speaks of hearing one of the colored preachers, "very ignorant

43 "In 1863 a member of the 51st Massachusetts Regiment sent this sketch to *Harper's Weekly* entitled 'The Effects of the Proclamation: Freed Negros Coming Into Our Lines at New Bern, North Carolina.'"

44. Edward Stowe Adams, 1873.

45. James Ford, Esq.

46. Reverend John Westall.

but eloquent" in a funeral discourse: "Now friends I reckon you all has sense enough to know that funeralizing don't do the dead no good—no—tain't no count to them what I say today—but the livin—thems the folks that needs the preaching." He spoke of the uncertainty of life and then shouted, "And worse for yese than all the rest, there'll be all dese yere tall white missionary teachers to ax you what you did with the eddication that they left home and friends and sojourned in warlike parts to give you and your children before you!" Several pages of philosophizing followed.

Enclosed in one of her letters was the original and translation of the first school composition written in the first Free School in Newbern by a former slave, twenty-five years of age.

She speaks of an evening class of ten colored soldiers who did guard duty at the prison. "One boy was asked if he didn't wish he was a Yankee. Replying, 'I mean to be one yet.' Yankee is their synonym for everything excellent."

Miss Betsey L. Canedy was transferred from Norfolk to Richmond, Virginia, and wrote:

> Our agent had hunted for a house but none could be found to rent to 'Nigger teachers' except outside the walls of the city and no land could be leased upon which to build as the N[ew] E[ngland] Society had intended a school room and living room over it. Finally one of the two brick buildings which had been used by the rebels during the war to manufacture ammunitions for their navy, which had been confiscated, was fitted up with rough boards for partitions—one sleeping room has straw beds on two settees—one iron bedstead filled with Government hay and briars. Six of us take meals in another building with the teachers of the white schools.

> Four hours of school in the morning and two hours in a night school. Schools are smaller than in the spring as the colored people have established schools with colored teachers in some localities.

Quoting from her letter of 1869: "After four years in Richmond the people generally are getting along comfortably and the rebels seem to feel less bitter than in the spring. The Freed people and real Union people have but little faith in their loyalty."

The assassination of President Abraham Lincoln on April 15, 1865, caused a sadness and gloom throughout the north unparalleled since, and which I can never forget although only a boy when Squire James Ford came home with the sad tidings [*Ford, who was an uncle of Mrs. Robert Adams, was residing with the Adams family*], soon followed by my father, Robert Adams, who at once took me down town where the streets were filled with anxious faces.

Leonard Wood (1805-1885) who had a store on Bedford Street [*Fruit and Nurseryman, 7 Bedford Street*] about where Clorite's fruit store now is, said, "it was the best news he had heard for forty years," whereupon men rushed into the store and upset everything, including the counters and stove. The police took Mr. Wood out by a rear window to the police station near, to save him from the infuriated crowd which quickly formed a procession and marched to the places of known copperheads [*a vocal faction of Democrats who were opposed to the Civil War, and wanted immediate peace with the Confederates*], and made them put out the United States flag – among those were Mark A. Slocum (1808-1876) on Third Street [*livery stable, 10 Third Street*] who had at one time been postmaster.

Reverend John Westall wrote a long poem, "In Memoriam," read before the Municipal Authorities and citizens of Fall River at the Memorial Services on the death of Abraham Lincoln, held in the City Hall on June 1, 1865, this was also published in pamphlet form.

Anne Chaloner Graves Canedy, (1821-1866)

Anne Chaloner Graves Canedy, a sister of Betsey Leonard Canedy, also resigned as a teacher in Fall River in 1863 and went south to teach. Extracts from her long letters give vivid descriptions of their nearness to the skirmishing lines as well as of the school work. Quoting in part from Newbern, May 1864:

> As I sit here, this same 5th of May 1864 the guns at Fort Spinola are banging away, shelling the woods beyond, and the other side, determined not to be outdone by Yankees, are banging back again. In other words we are 'attacked'; but as we have had raids, and attacks, and rams, and gunboats, and bomb shells, and in fact all of wars legion of horrors for our 'morning song and evening sacrifice' for the last two weeks, I have become, I am afraid, thoroughly hardened. I can't get up a particle of fear for myself. I feel anxious for the poor soldiers, on both sides, who are driven into this thing.

47. Anne Chaloner Graves Canedy "who resigned as a teacher [*in Fall River*] to take up teaching the freedmen at the south."

When we had an alarm in February, I was thoroughly frightened, and expected to be on my way to Richmond every day for a week, but now although the danger is said to be much greater, I am ready to meet it. I think if we are taken, I should rather enjoy the novelty of a trip to Libby Prison—<u>Friday morning</u>. The firing stopped last night at dark—a few shells were thrown during the night, but I didn't wake once. No one on our side was hurt. It is reported that the shells killed several rebels in the woods but nothing is yet known certainly. Today they have sent in a flag of truce, very respectfully asking for an <u>unconditional surrender</u>, which invitation was of course most politely declined. Major [*Thorndike Cleaves*] Jameson [*1814-1891*], one of the callers, says General [*William Jackson*] Palmer's [*1836-1909*] reply was, 'We cant see it. If you want Newbern come and take it. We'll give you just half an hour to clear out in.'

The reply or something else started them, for in a very few hours our cavalry had scoured the country for nine miles round and not a single 'butter nut' could be found. The boat for New York has been kept back for several days as it is not thought quite safe on the water yet, but here in town everything goes on just as usual. I think everyone feels perfectly safe, even if there should be a real attack. We think we could hold out against any force they will be able to bring. They cant do anything here without the ram, and she has got to overcome a multitude of obstacles before she can get here to operate.

I have been over the river today to see the Washington refugees —I wish I could describe this scene to you, but I have no pen that will do it.

In a letter of February, 1865, she said:

At the time the boxes arrived there had not been an article received at the distributing office for several months—not a garment could be begged or bought anywhere. Anything in the shape of bedclothes they are almost crazy to get as they suffer so much with the cold in their open cabins. You sent 183 articles.

Wish you could have seen the multitude that started from the church where my school is held on the morning of January 1st— they wanted a flag to 'rally round'—Miss Canedy used part of a childs red dress the only red that could be found in Newbern, for

48. Aerial view of Fall River, Massachusetts, looking north, late 1860s.

the white strips using part of an old sheet that came in one of the boxes, and for the blue bought cambric. The winter was cold and one day found fourteen who had neither shoes nor stockings.

After the afternoon session, I have a class of ten colored soldiers who do guard duty at the prison – one of the soldiers seemed in a hurry—on inquiry he wanted to teach his own school composed of 30 of his fellow soldiers. She asked a nine year old blackface boy, 'What do you mean to be?' 'A philosopher' was the cool reply —'What is that?' I asked? 'A man full of wisdom' was the reply.

Yankee, as previously mentioned, was their synonym for everything excellent.

While at Newbern, Miss Anne C. G. Canedy wrote of the teachers being sent to Beaufort, North Carolina, on account of war danger. "When their going was announced the older scholars seemed just ready to give up—none of them said much but all seemed to feel that they were lost. We

49. Azariah Shove Tripp.

who stayed back were advised to keep as close as possible as we were really disobeying orders from headquarters."

She quotes an old antiquated black man at a funeral, "Contrasting their present conditions with their former he said 'now my chilluns what would ye been if it wasn't for dese Yankies? Coz fore de Yankies took Newbern dar wasn't no men nor women—dar was nothing but slaves.' He prayed 'Oh Lord look out for Jeff Davis—let him see how bad he's situated.' He talked an hour as fast as he could speak and just as original as you can imagine. They are at times truly eloquent band some of their expressions are very beautiful."

"Today I have a school of 200 averaging 150 and one assistant, tomorrow I may have 250 and no help and next day I may have but 50 scholars and four assistants. How I should like to have Azariah [*Shove*] Tripp [*1826-1888*] here just one week. Wouldn't he straighten matters in short order." Azariah S. Tripp was a member of the School Committee when Miss Canedy taught in Fall River.

"I now have the best classes in the galleries of my church and my assistant has the little ones in the pews below."

She speaks of soldiers walking in saying:

> 'We are interested in your work and should like to visit the school awhile.' We of course have to be very glad to see them and entertain them as politely as we can and do what we can for them in the way of singing which let me assure you, is by no means a small affair. I don't believe there is a white school in all Yankeedom that can make as much music in a given time as mine can. They all sing from the four year olds to Uncle George, 'who is nigh eighty—Honey.'

> Then some women come in and ask, 'Have ye any letters from Wilde's Brigade?' [*Brigadier General Edward Augustus Wilde (1825-1891), known as Wilde's African Brigade.*] 'Have you one from my husband,' and I'll ask what name she wants it for— then she will answer, 'Well my husband's name is John Lewis and my name is Dinah Green but maybe he'd put Dinah Gaston on the outside of the letter, for that was my young mistress' name and the old master give me to her when he died. And if ye cant find nary one for me, pears like he must have written to Willie Smith—caze she's his cousin and he thinks a heap of her.' If I am fortunate enough to find a letter, I read it to her and then answer it—generally writing as they dictate and they almost invariably write them to keep praying.

A letter of February, 1865, spoke highly of the boxes of clothing from the Fall River Society. As soon as it became known of the arrival of the clothing, "there was a great demand as not a garment could be bought or begged anywhere and not an article had been received at the distributing office for several months.

"I have some idea of turning doctor and intend to write Boston this week for medicines—I have such frequent requests for something to cure, that I must have something to supply their demand," and enumerates some of the medicines they want for certain troubles, such as "ginger to cure a misery in the stomach," etc. … In the same long letter of seven, four-page sheets, filled with the conditions and problems and of "having moved into our new home," she then speaks of walking thru the refugee camp: "There are now in addition to those who were there before between 2 and 3 thousand from Washington and Plymouth. Every cabin was crowded before so they put up tents which were old condemned army tents full of holes and for a cook stove, dug a shallow hole in the ground and make a fire in the hole." Most of them left comfortable homes in Washington and took only such clothing and furniture as they could "tote."

Another who went from Fall River was Reverend Andrew Duncan Milne (1808-1866), a great uncle of Mr. John Tuttle Swift (1877-1940). After his ministry in Tiverton, Rhode Island, he went south in the interests of the freedmen, being located at St. Helena, Port Royal, South Carolina. During his stay there a number of boxes of clothing were sent from here. From 1864 to 1866, he was the editor of the *Fall River News*.

Following are three outstanding names of African Americans who accomplished so much for their people as to be recorded in encyclopedias and biographical dictionaries of whom I wish to speak and quote.

Harriet Tubman (c.1820-1914), a woman escaped from slavery in 1849, was considered "one of the most conspicuous figures in the work of the Underground Railroad, gaining the name of Moses." She spent one night "at a house behind shelves filled with boxes which made a false wall which slowly opened." She spoke at Anti-Slavery meetings and piloted slaves to Canada on nineteen trips and led away more than 300 slaves. During the Civil War, military officers granted her a free pass on all Government transports. She performed valuable services for the National Government as a spy, and as a nurse in hospitals.

A tablet of bronze erected in Auburn, New York, "In memory of Harriet Tubman," bears the following:

> On my underground railroad,
> I nebber run my train off de track
> An I nebber los a passenger.

Sojourner Truth [*born Isabella 'Bell' Baumfree (c.1797-1883)*], sold in slavery from her parents at the age of nine, "became a very famous lecturer, although untaught and illiterate, she is recorded as having a remarkable mind. At Anti-Slavery meetings she was one of the chief attractions—her shrewd good sense, oddities of speech, and whimsical illustrations coupled with deep religious conviction never failed to produce sympathetic interest." The following remark has often been quoted: "She knew the Bible only as it was read to her, but many times interrupted its reading to exclaim, 'Is dat in dar? I knew dat, God told me.'" She lectured in Fall River after the Civil War and spent nearly a week at the home of my father, Robert Adams.

Frederick Douglass [*born Frederick Augustus Washington Bailey (c.1818-1895)*] escaped from slavery in 1838, was aided in Philadelphia and New York, came to Newport and thence by stage to New Bedford became very active in the Anti-Slavery cause. His first lecture in Nantucket, Massachusetts, made so favorable an impression that he became an agent for the Massachusetts Anti-Slavery Society. He lectured in Fall River in 1848 at Union Hall, and several times later, also in many of the large cities and in England. He was closely identified with Charles Sumner and William Lloyd Garrison, and had interviews with President Abraham Lincoln, suggesting the use of black soldiers. Later he was appointed United States Minister to Haiti [*from 1889 to 1891*].

Frederick Douglass lectured many times in Fall River in Anti-Slavery days also during and after the Civil War. He became an intimate friend of my father Robert Adams during those years and spent the night at our house when lecturing in Fall River, and made a special visit to see my father about 1890. Mr. Douglass had a fine physique and was a delightful conversationalist.

The Frederick Douglass Memorial and Historical Society of New Bedford held a meeting in that city on September 18, 1938, in commemoration of the one hundredth anniversary of the escape of Frederick Douglass from slavery. References to his life were given in all the public schools of that city. He lived in New Bedford from 1838-1841.

50. Sojourner Truth: "President Lincoln gained much of his knowledge of slavery and its cruelties from her."

51. Frederick Douglass, "a personal friend of my father, stopping at our home when lecturing ... a man of commanding presence, an able speaker, and an enjoyable conversationalist."

AUTHOR'S NOTES

The various colonies existing in southern New England had customs which widely varied. Salem, Plymouth, Providence, and Portsmouth, although nearby in distance, were widely separated in modes of living, but slavery was then accepted and even exploited by the most righteous citizens of each community.

Slavery in the colonies followed the customs then existing in the mother country. Foes taken in war were ordinarily sold to foreign bondage. In order that prisoners might be held for ransom or sold, the horrible massacres on early battlefields were greatly mitigated. King Charles II (1630-1685) marketed his Scottish subjects. James II (1633-1701) sold 841 Englishmen whom he had captured in the Monmouth Rebellion [*aka The Revolt of the West, or The West Country Rebellion, March–July, 1685.*] (See Goodwin page 562).

Prior to the landing of the Pilgrims an English captain, Thomas Hunt (c.1594-1666) captured twenty-seven Indians on the New England coast and carried them to England as slaves. In 1638, Captain William Peirce (c.1580-1656) took Pequot Indians to the West Indies and "brought back negro slaves." In 1648 the second *Mayflower* was engaged in the slave trade. (See Goodwin p. 156 and p. 472).

For many years of early local colonial history, the territory now occupied by Fall River was in Plymouth Colony but it was not settled by the colonists. The territory from Freetown bounds on the north to Puncatest, near the Little Compton, Rhode Island, line on the south, and from Dartmouth, Massachusetts, bounds, including all of the Watuppa ponds on the east, to and including Warren, Rhode Island, on the west, was occupied by the Indians, and no white men settled there until after the Indian War [*King Philip's War, June 20, 1675–April 12, 1678*]. Included in this territory was what is now Bristol, Rhode Island, which had been settled by colonists from Boston. Bristol was then a county seat, and

Bristol County included the Fall River territory and the towns around it. Portsmouth, Rhode Island (then called Pocasset), was settled by fugitives from Boston in 1638. These settlers in Portsmouth gradually extended their holdings to include land around Newport, Rhode Island. Some land in Tiverton and at Nanaquaket came under this claim of ownership. Fall River social habits were very much influenced by those which prevailed in Warren and in Newport, as these were the nearest settlements, the towns and places to and from which our paths or roads led. Most of the land in Fall River was purchased by or for those who had first settled in Portsmouth [*the Freeman's Purchase, June 10, 1686*], and they and their servants and slaves tilled the land and gradually occupied it when it was divided at the close of the Indian War.

Both Bristol and Newport were prominent as centers of the slave trade. By 1739, Newport had become a leading slave mart. Its first shipment of slaves came in 1696 from Africa, and its men and women were disposed of at from $150 to $175 each. Between that date and 1708, there was no demand for slaves, but Rhode Island men soon realized that there was a fortune in the triangular business of rum, sugar and slaves. Ships sailed from Newport to Africa with rum, exchanged the rum for slaves, and then sailed to the Barbados where the slaves were exchanged for sugar and molasses, which in turn were brought back to Newport for the manufacture of more rum. Newport residents operated more than twenty distilleries for this trade. The ships would sail with a hundred or more hogsheads of rum and with that they would buy more than a hundred slaves, purchasing them from the native chieftains in Africa. Then, at the Barbados, West Indies, they would sell the slaves at a profit of from sixty to one hundred and twenty-five dollars each and invest the proceeds in sugar and molasses, so that a voyage often netted a ship-owner $10,000.

Between 1739 and 1760, the slave trade boomed. When the American Revolution began, it broke up the triangular slave trade, and in 1774 Rhode Island passed a law prohibiting the importation of slaves. In 1787, the Rhode Islanders were forbidden to engage in the foreign slave trade.

Pierce's history of Freetown [A History of the Town of Freetown, *by Palo Alto Pierce (1853-1931)*] says that before the Indian War slavery was countenanced in Freetown by all classes, both of church and state. The family invested in "negro boys and girls" to the extent of their means, using them almost entirely for farm labor or for house servants. Slave trade was discontinued at the beginning of the American Revolution because the British cruisers laid in wait along the coast for all small American vessels. In 1783, Massachusetts courts rendered a decision which outlawed this trade, but slavery continued. The churches had black pews, the burial grounds had graves set apart for them, and they were frequently mentioned in wills. For instance, in 1754, Jacob Hathaway, Sr. (1675-1759) willed "three negro boys and four negro girls." Congress forbade all African slave trade in 1807.

Bristol, our shire town, was very prominent in slave trade. Taking from Munro's history of the town [The History of the Town of Bristol, R.I., *by Wilfred Harold Munro (1849-1934)*], we find that Colonel Nathaniel Byfield (1653-1733), a leading citizen, by will allowed in 1733, freed his slave "Rose." He had brought her to Bristol in 1718. In 1730, Reverend John Usher (1695-1775) objected to his parishioners [*at St. Michael's Episcopal Church, founded in 1719*] because he was not allowed to "baptize negroes" who attended his church.

In 1767, the town of Bristol was disturbed because Indian and black servants or slaves were "out at unseasonable hours of the night," and voted that an officer be appointed to put the curfew law in effect. The census of 1738 shows one hundred twenty-eight colored persons in the town. This included thirteen Indians. The census of 1785 disclosed "seventy-three slaves, twenty-five free negroes and twenty-four Indians and other servants," a total of one-hundred-twenty-two domestics. There were one hundred twenty-six dwelling houses in the town at that time, and two hundred and eighteen distinct families.

In the slave trade, the number of people carried in each boat was not large. In a letter to Capt. James De Wolfe (1764-1837) in 1796, his ship captain, Jeremiah Diman (1770-1833), reported from St. Thomas, Virgin Islands, that he had arrived there with seventy-eight slaves, and was selling them for about twenty-five joes ($200) each. In four years, over twelve thousand people were delivered to slave merchants in the vicinity of Charleston, and two-thirds of these were landed from Rhode Island vessels. Four thousand slaves came from Bristol ships and thirty-five hundred from Newport ships.

African slaves were largely purchased from tribal chieftains (inland tribes) and had been captured by them in tribal wars. But for their money value many of these would have been slain.

It is thus seen that when the Federal Constitution was formed, the importation of slaves was greatly curtailed. The South was the slave-holding country and the substantial wealth arising from the sales of the slaves was the basis of many of the large fortunes of the leading families who were our neighbors. Yet even the slave-holding was controversial —soon laws prohibited the importation of slaves in Massachusetts (no person could be born into slavery or imported as a slave). The South of course insisted on the continuance of the custom and no federation of the states would have been possible had not slave rights been incorporated into our Constitution.

"Arthur Sherman Phillips, Esq. (1865-1941), has added the following items":

CONSTITUTION OF THE UNITED STATES
Article IV, Section 2, Clause 3

"No person held to Service or Labour in one State, under the laws thereof, and escaping into another shall be discharged from such Service of Labour, but shall be delivered up, on claim of the party to whom such Service or Labour may be due".

The United States Supreme Court, sustaining this law, ruled in 1872 that "without this provision the Union could not have been formed." See: Osborn vs Nicholson 13 Wallace (United States Supreme Court), p. 66.

Under Act of Congress passed in 1793, a person entitled to Labor or Service of another, was empowered to seize the fugitive, take him before a Federal Court or any local magistrate, and upon proof satisfactory to the magistrate, either by oral evidence or by affidavit—that the labour or Service was due, and upon a certificate thereof issued by the Court, such certificate warranted a removal of the fugitive to the place from which he had fled. This Act was held constitutional in 1842. See: Prigg vs Pennsylvania 16 Peters (United States Supreme Court) p. 616.

The Fugitive Slave law did not apply where a master took his slave into a free state nor when an arrested fugitive, who was (after public notice) sold in the Free State for the benefit of his owner.

52. Reverend Joshua Young D.D.

Supplement

Reverend Joshua Young D.D.
(1823-1904)

Joshua Young was born in East Pittsfield, Maine, on September 29, 1823, the son of Aaron Young (1783-1875) and his wife, née Mary Coburn (1780-1866). In 1827, the Young family moved to Bangor, Maine, where Joshua was educated in the public schools, being prepared for college at the Bangor high school. He entered Bowdoin College in Brunswick, Maine, graduating with the class of 1845, after which he entered the divinity school at Harvard University, graduating in 1848. He was awarded a Doctor of Divinity by Bowdoin in 1890.

He was ordained on February 1, 1849 at the New North Church in Boston, and, ten days later, married Mary Elizabeth Plympton (1825-1912), a member of an old and esteemed family of Cambridge, Massachusetts; the couple celebrated their Golden Wedding Anniversary fifty years later. Reverend Young was appointed pastor at the New North Church that same year, serving that congregation until May, 1852, when he resigned his post. Several pastorates followed: Burlington, Vermont, from December 16, 1852, to May 29, 1862; Deerfield, Massachusetts, for a brief stint in 1862; and Hingham, Massachusetts, from October 1, 1863, to December 20, 1868.

He was next called to serve at the Unitarian Church in Fall River, Massachusetts, where he relocated with his wife and children; ministering to that congregation from December 27, 1868 to early March, 1875. The Young family resided on Maple Street, and quickly became part of the community, the introduction eased, no doubt, through the auspices of prominent friends and associates made during their abolitionist activities. Rev. Young earned the esteem of his parishioners and other city residents, forming new friendships that would last the remainder of his life.

His longest pastorate was at the First Parish Unitarian Church in Groton, Massachusetts, where he served from March 7, 1875 to March 1, 1902, at which time he resigned from active pastoral work, being unanimously elected Pastor Emeritas.

In June, 1902, the Young's relocated to Winchester, Massachusetts, "that [they] might live their remaining years in the vicinity of [their] children and grandchildren." The couple were the parents of five children: Mary Elizabeth Young (1849-1891), the wife of Daniel Stevens; Grace Desoe Young (1851-1901), the wife of John Frederick Patten; Lucy Florence Young (1854-1922); Joshua Edson Young (1857-1940); and Henry Guy Young (1865-1936).

Rev. Young spent his final years engaged in literary endeavors, some of which were published nationally, and actively pursued "things that tended to promote ... moral and intellectual growth" of his community. He preached the final sermon of his distinguished career during the Christmas service at the First Parish Unitarian Church in Groton on December 20, 1903, having been invited by his former parishioners as guest preacher.

He died at his residence at Winchester, Massachusetts on February 7, 1904, and was eulogized as a man of "commanding presence, gracious manners ... the able preacher, the good citizen, and the Christian gentleman."

The Youngs were extremely sympathetic to the abolitionist cause; shortly after their marriage and during their residency in Boston, they became involved in the Underground Railroad, sheltering runaway slaves in their residence. By the time they settled in Burlington, they had become increasingly active participants; that town served as an important location for fugitive slaves on the path to freedom in Canada. Due to the very public aspect of his pastorate, and with parishioners frequently calling at his residence, Rev. Young ceased secreting fugitive slaves in his parsonage, instead sheltering them in the barn on the property. Mrs. Young steadfastly assisted in the endeavor, believing herself to be less high profiled in the community and, therefore, less suspect. It is uncertain when he made the acquaintance of Mrs. William Buffington Chace, née Elizabeth Buffum, and her abolitionist family and friends in Fall River, but during his pastorate in Burlington, he and Mrs. Young were assisting the former in their Underground Railroad activities.

Rev. Young was incensed at the treatment of Anthony Burns, an escaped slave from Virginia who was returned south from Boston, Massachusetts in shackles in 1854, due to the Fugitive Slave Act. His response: preaching blistering sermons, denouncing the ruling as "wicked

53. Mrs. Reverend Joshua Young, née Mary Elizabeth Plympton.

54. Unitarian Church, Fall River, Massachusetts; Reverend Young served this congregation from December 27, 1868, to early March, 1875.

55. First Parish Unitarian Church, Groton, Massachusetts; Reverend Young served this congregation from March 7, 1875, to March 1, 1902. The Youngs' High Street residence is depicted at the left.

56. Rev. and Mrs. Young in the "Study in [*the*] High Street house. Groton, Mass."

and infamous." His deep belief in the evils of slavery and the necessity of its abolition intensified in the ensuing years.

He admired the radically controversial abolitionist John Brown, who went to extreme in his desire to free those enslaved, culminating in his ill-fated attempt on October 16, 1859, to incite a violent revolt at Harpers Ferry, [West] Virginia. Brown was apprehended, brought to trial for treason, and sentenced to death; he was executed at Charles Town, Virginia, on December 2, 1859. The sensational events captured the attention of the nation, and the drama was followed with rapt attention.

Rev. Young was among those who sympathized, and believed Brown a martyr to the abolitionist cause; he hastened with a friend through a stormy night, intent on attending the funeral at North Elba, New York. He arrived on December 8, 1859, a few hours before the commencement of the service, and, finding himself the only member of the clergy present, complied with an impromptu request from Wendell Phillips, who asked him to officiate at the funeral.

A prayer was offered by Rev. Young, followed by what he later described as a "matchless speech" by Wendell Phillips. As the body was lowered into the grave, the reverend delivered the following: "I have fought a good fight, I have finished my course, I have kept thy faith. Henceforth there is laid up for me a crown of righteousness which the righteous judge shall give me at that day, and not to me only, but unto all them also that love his appearing" [2 Timothy 4:7-8].

"The Funeral of John Brown," written by Rev. Young offers a comprehensive telling of his participation in the event; the article was published in New England Magazine, Vol. XXX, No. 2 in April, 1904.

For his part in the drama, Young was lauded by some, and scorned by others, the latter including several influential members of his Burlington congregation; some left immediately in indignation, and others, more gradually. The contempt and social ostracism subsequently levied on him and his family prompted his resignation. In his letter of resignation he wrote: "I rejoice that no graver charge is made against me than that I have pushed the principals of general justice and benevolence too far, further than cautious policy would warrant and further than the feelings of some would go along with me. In every accident which may happen through life, in pain and sorrow, in depression, in distress, I will call to mind this accusation and be comforted."

Strong words, indeed.

On August 30, 1899, Reverend Young again participated in a burial that took place on John Brown's farm in North Elba. In July of that year, what became known as the "second raid on Harpers Ferry" took place. Three men—Dr. Thomas Featherstonhaugh (c.1850-1920), Captain E.P. Hall of Washington, DC, and Dr. Orin Grant Libby (1864-1952), a history professor from the University of Wisconsin—disinterred the remains of the eight men who were killed during the 1859 raid. Their intention was to secretly transport them to North Elba where they would be reinterred beside Brown's gravesite. [*The eight men were: Oliver Brown (1839-1859); John Henry Kagi (1835-1859); Lewis Sheridan Leary (1835-1859); William Henry Leeman (1839-1859); Dangerfield Newby (1815-1859); Stewart Taylor (1836-1859); Dauphin Adolphus Osgood Thompson (1838-1859); and William Thompson (1833-1859).*]

Once in New York, photographer Katherine Elizabeth McClellan (1859-1934) enlisted a local undertaker to have the remains prepared for reburial. She also headed the committee that planned the event, which was attended by 3,000 people.

At her request, as well as members of Brown's family, Rev. Young officiated at the ceremony and delivered the benediction.

The following article, "The Funeral of John Brown," was written by Rev. Joshua Young later in his life. His original handwritten manuscript, together with a period typewritten transcript, are contained in an archive of Young family material held in the Charlton Library of Fall River History at the Fall River Historical Society; this version is published here for the first time.

The Funeral of John Brown

It happened to the writer of this paper, on the 8th of December, 1859, to stand in the shadow of a great solitary rock in the wilderness of the Adirondack Mountains, and see committed to the grave, with the usual rites of honorable burial, the body of one who but six days before, 'neath the distant skies of Virginia, was swinging on a gibbet convicted by the court that tried him with indecent haste, of treason, conspiracy with slaves to rebel and murder in the first degree. It was a scene of touching pathos, of unutterable emotion. Across the wintry sky, clouds were sailing like the swift ships. All around stood the deep primeval forest bending to the western winds, while in the near distance, capped with snow, loomed the everlasting hills, grand and solemn; mingling the sublimity of nature with the moral grandeur of an immortal deed. It was the old, old story of the prophet's fate:

> Truth forever on the scaffold, wrong forever on the throne,
> But the scaffold sways the future
> And behind the dim unknown
> Standeth God, beyond the shadow, keeping
> Watch above his own.

In less than two years thereafter, the name John Brown became a nation's epic and gave to an army song with little merit in itself either of sentiment or expression. An influence for patriotism in the mighty struggle that ensued for the nation's life, hardly inferior to that which was exerted, during the French Revolution, by the famous Marseillaise. His heroic embrace of death in behalf of a despised and oppressed race, roused from fatal slumber a nation's conscience, thrilled all liberty-loving hearts the whole world over, and inaugurated on this western continent a resolution of such magnitude as the world never saw before. It struck the death knell of chattel slavery within the Union, and swept from the face of the earth the cruelest oppression that ever revealed the pitiless contempt of the strong for the weak.

What is familiarly known as John Brown's Raid at Harpers Ferry had, if we may believe the martyr's own word, and that is not for a moment to be doubted, a two-fold object; first to run off slaves, flee with them to the pastures of the near wooded heights, and thence to Canada; second, to strike terror to the hearts of the Slave-holding States.

Of its disastrous failure, of the fierce conflict that ensued in which nearly all of the little band of invaders were either killed or wounded, and the leader himself captured, blood flowing from six ghastly wounds, and thought to be dying, and his sons lying dead by his side, of this the astonishing story may be found in any one of the several lives of John Brown to be found in every town library. [*The sons were Oliver Brown (1839-1859), who was killed at Harpers Ferry on October 17, 1859, and Watson Brown (1835-1859), who was wounded at Harpers Ferry and died two days later on October 19, 1859.*] The object of this paper is to complete the wonderful story, to follow the dead body of the hero to its last resting place in the heart of the Adirondacks, describe the scenes that occurred on its five days' passage from Harpers Ferry to North Elba, and thus to contribute to history an authentic account of the Burial of John Brown; and incidentally, to submit an explanation of the humble part taken by the writer in the solemn rites that closed one of the most remarkable chapters in American history.

But first, to remove a suspicion that seems to lurk in the minds of some who ask, why or how it was that Brown's habitation was so far removed from what may be called the theatre of his public life, as if at that time he were in hiding like a guilty thing—a simple statement will not only answer this question but will increase our admiration of this remarkable man.

Gerrit Smith [*(1797-1874)*], a noted New York abolitionist and philanthropist, to whom that territory belonged, had set apart a certain portion of it for the benefit of such colored persons, especially fugitive slaves, as would go there and establish homes. John Brown bought a farm near by, and thereon erected a small one-story-and-a-half cottage, unfinished at the time of the raid, that he might give to these untrained colonists the benefit of his experience and counsel as a pioneer farmer and keeper of herds.

The second day of December dawned in New England in cold and darkness. All day black clouds drifted before the wind. From morning to night a dismal drizzling rain fell. But in the lull of the storm was heard the funeral knell. Men met and passed, sad and silent, or if they stopped to speak, the one topic on the street was the tragedy at Charlestown. In all the principal towns of the northern states, services of a religious character were held, in New Bedford, Worcester, Providence, Plymouth, Portland, Concord. In New York a prayer meeting was held in Dr. Cheever's church [*Rev. Dr. George Barrell Cheever (1907-1890), Church of the Puritans,*] and a great meeting in Philadelphia, at which Dr. Turner offered prayer, and Lucretia Mott [*née Coffin (1793-1880)*], Ednah Cheney [*Mrs. Seth Wells Cheney, née Ednah Dow Littlehale (1824-1904)*] and other noble women spoke, often interrupted with hisses, was almost broken up by a respectable mob. In Washington the tolling of the historic bell cast in Paul Revere's foundry was stopped by orders from the White House. In Boston a vast assembly filled the Tremont Temple, the walls of which were covered with mottoes, sayings of Washington, Lafayette and John Brown; Gov. John A. Andrew [*John Albion Andrew (1818-1867), 25th Governor of Massachusetts, in office January 1861-January 1866]*, presided and speeches, having no uncertain sound, were made by Rev. J.M. Manning [*Rev. Jacob Merrill Manning (1824-1882)]* of the Old South [*Church, Boston, Massachusetts*], Ralph Waldo Emerson [*(1803-1882)]* and Wendell Phillips [*(1811-1884)]*. The Rev. Dr. Rollins H. Neale [*Rev. Dr. Rollin Herber Neale (1808-1879), pastor of the First Baptist Church, Boston, Massachusetts]* offered prayer. The stores of the colored citizens on Brattle Street were closed and draped. Nor did this groundswell of public agitation stop here. It struck the shores of England and France, and called forth from that exiled patriot and prophet-poet in his island home, Victor Hugo [*Victor-Marie Hugo (1802-1885)]*, an impassioned appeal to the American people: "I fall on my knees weeping before the great star-spangled banner of the New World, and with clasped hands and with profound and filial respect, I implore the illustrious American Republic to see to the safety of the universal Moral Law, to save John Brown. O let America know and ponder on it well, there is something more terrible than Cain slaying Abel; it is Washington slaying Spartacus!"

In Virginia the sun rose clear and bright on the second of December. A haze that presently veiled it, soon disappeared, and before the hour appointed for the hero's death, not a cloud was to be seen. The temperature was mild and genial that until late in the afternoon the windows of all the houses were open, while the glittering blades and bayonets of regiments of soldiers on foot and on horses, called out to guard against an attempt to rescue the doomed man—such was the consternation of the people—would have suggested to a casual observer, but for the absence of the usual crowd of spectators, the going on of an impressive military parade.

Examined and pronounced dead by the physicians in attendance, the body was cut down and placed in a coffin. The Cavalry, wheeling aside closed in around the wagon into which it was lifted, and marched back to the jail.

Later in the afternoon, at about four o'clock, as the clouds of an approaching storm began to gather in the sky, as if nature herself were touched with the great sorrow, the body was conveyed to the railroad station and thence to Harpers Ferry, under a strong military escort, and delivered to the weeping wife [*Mrs. John Brown, née Mary Ann Day (1816-1884)]* and friends to be taken North.

The next morning the mournful journey began; and strange is the story to be told of its passage through shuddering cities to the distant wilderness.

The papers having announced that the body of John Brown would arrive in Philadelphia on Saturday at noon, a large crowd assembled at the station on Broad and Prime Streets, most of whom were colored people and so pressed into the building, interrupting the business of the place, that the officers had to exclude them. Tender and sensitive they bore this with difficulty.

A committee of fifty men appointed at a meeting in Shiloh, colored church, arrived at the depot about twelve o'clock, and not being able to get admittance to the building stationed themselves on the opposite side of the Street. They were dressed in black and had come to serve as an escort or company of pall bearers, while the body was being taken to its temporary resting place in the city.

On the arrival of the train, the excitement outside the station increased and persons pushed their way through the fence to get if but a peep at the coffin-box. Mrs. Brown, accompanied by Mr. Hector Tyndale [*(1821-1880), later a Brigadier General*], walked quietly through the crowd without being recognized, and took passage in the Eleventh Street car for the house of a friend. The party having charge of the body had telegraphed from Baltimore to have a wagon at the station for the purpose of conveying the body to an undertaker's where it was to be embalmed, placed in another coffin, and kept until Monday morning.

Immediately on the arrival of the train the Mayor [*Alexander Henry (1823-1883), 69th mayor of Philadelphia, in office May, 1858–January, 1865*] attended by several policemen appeared upon the scene, entered the car and objected to this proceeding, and insisted that the body should be taken directly through the city. The committee, of which Dr. Turner was one, remonstrated; it was an amazing exercise of authority; Mrs. Brown was sick and required rest. Still the Mayor insisted and, calling their attention to the increased excitement and the divided state of public opinion, informed the committee that the peace of the city was more important than the accommodation they asked for. He would hold himself responsible to have the body carefully taken across the city to the New York station at two o'clock.

The time was short, and there was great danger of a painful scene. The Mayor, to quiet the tumult of the people and still the clamor of the outside, crowd resorted to strategy.

There was in the car a long tool box. This he took and wrapped around it a deerskin also found in the car, so as to make it look like a coffin. The crowd in the station was then forced back and this box was conveyed carefully to a wagon on the shoulders of six policemen.

"Silent like men in solemn haste." The wagon left the yard and was driven in the direction of the Anti-slavery office, where it was said the body could lie in state, followed by the colored crowd almost in a state of frenzy. The station thus cleared of people another wagon backed up to the side door, into which was put a plain pine box containing the real body. It was then driven out of the station by the northern gate and down to Walnut Street wharf, where it was lifted into one of the baggage crates, and again placed in charge of Mr. J. M. McKim, [*Rev. James Miller McKim (1821-1880)*] who immediately proceeded with it to New York, there to await the coming of Mrs. Brown on Monday.

With all the precaution possible to avoid publicity and save a repetition of a similar scene, the coffin was taken to an undertaker's room on the Bowery. All day Sunday the newspaper reporters were sorely puzzled to ascertain the whereabouts of the body and it was quite midnight before they were able "to light upon it," nevertheless the gentlemen of the press insisted that the party having it in charge should get up and "show them the elephant." Remonstrance was in vain; the whole press gang were admitted to where the body lay; the coffin and its contents thereupon underwent a close and critical examination, and the result was spread out in full in the morning papers. Which called forth from one of the more respectable journals the remark: "Henceforth let no one say the Vampyre is a fiction."

The next state in the mournful journey was Troy. The little cortege guarding the precious body reached that city at two o'clock on Monday afternoon, and stopped at the American House. The American House was a temperance hotel and had been Capt. Brown's usual stopping place when in that city, he himself being a total abstainer from all intoxicating drinks, and also from tobacco in any form, and it may likewise be said of him that he was never heard to use a profane word, nor did he allow it to be used by any of his company. Like Joan of Arc he made all his soldiers leave off swearing and go to praying. His general appearance was that of a clergyman. He was a remarkable example of personal neatness and natural refinement.

At ten o'clock the next morning, Tuesday, the party had reached Vergennes in the state of Vermont, having spent the night in Rutland, where they received every attention. The news spread like wildfire; immediately the hotel was crowded with the leading citizens of the place who came to express their respect and sympathy.

Carriages were provided in which to convey the body and the party accompanying it to the lake shore, and a procession was formed in part of the hotel, noiselessly, and when the hour came to start all moved forward amid the tolling of solemn bells.

At the lake shore—Lake Champlain—a boat was in readiness, which, deflecting from its usual course, landed them by the town of Westport, and thus accelerated them on their mournful journey. Mrs. Brown was now among the friends and familiar acquaintances of her husband, and every kindness which the occasion called for was freely bestowed.

At this point properly enters the story of my personal connection with the ceremonies of John Brown's burial, which my friends have persistently urged me to tell.

My hesitation to do so is overcome only by the fact that in this way, as can be done in no other so well, I can transport you back a whole generation, reproduce the past as in a picture, and show you the times of my story as they were.

I am entitled to no merit for the humble part I took. I did not seek it, neither could I decline it.

I had no personal acquaintance with John Brown, had never seen his face nor heard his voice save as it was in the air in those days of anti-slavery struggle. I only knew him as a mighty man of valor in defense of endangered liberty, the liberator of Kansas. John Brown of Ossawatomie, a man fired with a great passion of humanity, an abolitionist from his youth up, the son of an abolitionist, a lineal descendant too of Peter Brown, the car porter who came over in the *Mayflower*.

"Ship of faith's last hope", and as such I honored and admired the man more than I can tell. Bred myself in the Garrisonian School of Abolitionist with an experience not accorded to all, being a member of the Vigilance Committee in Boston, for the protection of fugitive slaves before the passage of the infamous Fugitive Slave Bill, and eye-witness of the rendition of Anthony Burns, a station keeper on the underground railroad, of course, when that blow at Harpers Ferry shook the whole nation like an earthquake, and all the world wondered, and men turned and looked at one another. I was one of the same, and being then an enthusiastic young man of only thirty-six years of age, it was easy to be imprudent and do what so many told me afterwards was very imprudent: "I had ruined all my professional prospects."

I was then pastor, in the seventh year of my ministry, of the Unitarian Church in Burlington, Vermont, situated on the shore of Lake Champlain, across which you see in the distance the misty peaks of the Adirondacks (John Brown's mountain home) a daily spectacle of beauty and grandeur.

For some days conflicting statements were made as to by what route the hero's body would be taken to its last resting place.

On Wednesday, just after dinner, I met on the street my parishioner and warm personal friend, an abolitionist like myself, only more ardent, Mr. Lucius Bigelow [*Lucius Henry Bigelow (1841-1916)*], who at once said to me, it is now known that the body of John Brown will cross the lake at Vergennes. I want exceedingly to go to his funeral, only say you will go with me as my companion and my guest, and we will take the next train. To whom I replied—I will meet you at the station at four o'clock.

When we arrived at Vergennes the threatening storm (It had been drizzling all day) had begun. It was pouring hard, with every prospect of a north-easter. To our inquiries, the answer came that the funeral procession had crossed the lake the evening before and must be now near its destination.

Confident that we could overtake it before it reached North Elba, or at any rate get there in season for the funeral services, we lost no time in hiring a driver to take us to the ferry in the township of Paton, six miles distant. We lost no time in making known to the ferryman our object, and great desire to be landed as soon as possible, on the further shore, Baker's Point. He shook his head at our request and at once gave us to understand that his license as a ferryman did not require him to cross the lake at so late an hour and in such a storm, and moreover that in his opinion John Brown deserved the fate which had befallen him. "Why," said one of us "do you know any evil of him." "No but a great deal of good. I knew John Brown well, he has crossed this ferry with me a hundred times, and a more honest, upright fair man does not exist; we all like him but he has no business meddling with the niggers." Our hearts sank like lead. Oh! How we did plead with that man to convert him. One hour went by, and two and three and yet there was no softening of that rock, no relenting. Suddenly there was a brightness outside the window of the dimly lighted room, and on going to the door lo! The wind had veered to the west, the clouds had broken up, and all around the darkness was disappearing. Surprised and excited I rushed back, exclaiming: "The stars in their courses fought against Sisera." See Mr. Ferryman, God's full-orbed moon has thrown a bridge of silver across the lake; he bids us go, and who shall hinder. To my unutterable joy as well as amazement, he said, "well I will call may man and if he will get up and help me we will see what we can do." In a few minutes we were at the shore. It was growing very cold and beginning to freeze.

The ferry-boat was a large scow with a mast on one side. The wet sail had already become as stiff as sheet-iron, and it was with much difficulty that we hoisted it to its place on the creaking mast. Before a strong wind we made the passage of three miles in good time, and at once the boat put back, leaving us, cold and more or less drenched with the flying spray, on an utterly unknown shore. We climbed the bank. It was past midnight—What next? Yonder we saw a glimmering light. We hailed as a bright propitious star, and such it proved. Knocking at the door, at once a young man, all dressed, as if he were expecting some one, appeared. "John Brown's funeral." We want some one to take us to Elizabethtown, if no further. "I will, if father is willing." Father was willing, and in less time than I can repeat the pious sentiment that came to my mind:

"The Lord will provide"

We were putting the ten miles to Elizabethtown behind us with as rapid pace as the roads would permit. We reached there about ten o'clock in the morning. But we were yet far behind; probably the body had already reached its destination; there was no time to lose. We waited only long enough to change horses; meanwhile we learned that, on the arrival of the party at Elizabethtown, which is the seat of justice for Essex County, N.Y. the court house was at once offered as a place in which to deposit the body for the night. In a few minutes, raining as it was, a respectable procession was formed and the body borne thither. Six young men took it upon themselves to sit up all night in the court house as a guard of honor, while another volunteered to start off on a swift horse to notify the anxious family of the party's approach. Our next stage on this strange ride was the valley of Keene where we entered a region of the grandest and most majestic scenery to be found any where in the Adirondack country. We had come to what is known as "Indian Pass," a ravine or gorge formed by close and parallel walls of nearly perpendicular cliffs, quite 2000 feet in height, and almost black in color. Through this and past the untamed forests that clothed the slopes beyond, we made our way along a mere cart-road, over rocks, over stumps; and we cling hard to our seats, lest the swaying of the wagon from side to side, pitching like a ship in a heavy sea, or its frequent plunge from a surmounted stump, should throw us out. For the great current of summer travel had not then begun to move into those regions.

O what a night was that! On such an errand! The great mountains and the deep woods and the awful silences, and the scudding clouds and the rolling moon with intervals of shadow, weird and spectral.

The day was breaking cold and clear, when we came out upon a broad table-land, across which the piercing winds swept, unhindered, and once more a pace faster than walking was possible. Soon we crossed a bridge spanning a brawling stream, worked our way up the long sandy road cut through the overhanging bluff, turned to the left, entered another long stretch of somber forest and, finally, emerged into an opening, a mere clearing in the woods, and right before us in the near distance stood the humble home of the heroic martyr, solitary amidst the "solitude that had taught him how to die."

We entered the house stiff in every limb. I might say half frozen and glad enough to feel the genial heat of the small stove around which we formed ourselves a part of a very considerable company of people, mostly friends and neighbors who had personally known and admired the man who had gone forth from them, a simple shepherd, and had come back dead, with a fame gone out into all the world.

Presently Mr. Wendell Phillips came into the room; a few words were exchanged, and then retiring for a few minutes, he returned and said to me—"Mr. Young you are a minister, admiration for this dead and sympathy with this bereaved family must have brought you here journeying all night through the cold rain and over the dismal mountains to reach the place. It would give Mrs. Brown and the other widows great satisfaction if you would perform the burial services of a clergyman on this occasion." Of course there was but one answer to make to such a request—and from that moment I knew why God had sent me there. For it must be remembered that five households and four families of North Elba were stricken by that blow at Harpers Ferry.

The funeral took place at one o'clock. The services began with a hymn which had been a favorite with Mr. Brown and with which he had successively sung all his children to sleep.

> Blow ye the trumpet, blow!
> The gladly solemn sound.
> Let all the nations know
> To earth's remotest bound,
> The year of jubilee has come.

It was sung to the good old tune of Lenox. It was at once recognized by all who knew anything about the old fashioned music, and all who could sing joined in, while heard above all the rest were the plaintive voices of the deeply moved negroes who constituted quite one half of the company, most of them fugitive slaves. After the hymn followed the prayer. It was a spontaneous offering, so the papers said at the time and remarkably consonant with the spirit of the occasion. It was reported in full in the *New-York Tribune*. I only know I prayed. Then followed one of Wendell Phillips' matchless speeches. Never were his lips of music more eloquent with tenderness and sympathy. It would almost have made you weep your eyes out to have heard him, and when, from addressing the weeping widows and fatherless children, he rose on the very wings of inspiration, into some sublime passage of description and prophecy. You would have felt, no, you would have seen a great vision, and never have forgotten it. It was more than a Mark Anthony over more than a Caesar's dead body.

Another hymn was then sung, during which the coffin was placed on a table before the door with face exposed so that all could see it. It was almost as natural as life, far more so than an ordinary corpse. There was a flush on the face, resulting from the peculiar mode of his death, and nothing of the pallor that is usual when life is extinct. Then followed the short procession from the house to the grave which was dug at the base of a great picturesque rock about fifty feet from the house, by the side of which already reposed, removed from their original resting-place in Connecticut, the remains of his grandfather, Capt. John Brown, a revolutionary soldier who died from exhaustion in actual service.

The procession was in the following order: The coffin borne by six young men, residents of the little hamlet, then Mrs. John Brown, supported by Mr. [*Wendell*] Phillips, then the widow of Oliver [*Brown, née Martha Evelyn Brewster (1842-1860)*] leaning on the arm of Mr. McKim [*Rev. James M. McKim*], who, in the other hand held that of the little girl Ellen [*Ellen Brown (1854-1917), later Mrs. James Beatty Fablinger*]; next the widow of Watson Brown [*née Isabella Thompson (1837-1907), later Mrs. Salmon Brown*] supported by myself; followed by the widow of William Thompson [*née Mary Elizabeth Brown (1841-1924)*], on the arm of my friend, Mr. [*Lucius H.*] Bigelow. [*William P. Thompson, the brother-in-law of Watson Brown, was killed at Harpers Ferry; his widow remarried three times, and was subsequently: Mrs. Jacob Harding; Mrs. George Walter Clapp; and Mrs. Archibald Richard Adair III.*]

As the body was lowered into the grave, the first gush of grief, apparently beyond control, burst from the family, then it was that there came to my lips the triumphant words of Paul, when according to tradition, brought before Nero, just before his death:—"I have fought a good fight,

I have finished my course, I have kept the faith. Henceforth there is laid up for me a crown of righteousness, which the righteous judge shall give me at that day: and not to me only, but unto all them also that love his appearing;" for which utterance at the grave of a "felon" I received again and again "the deserved rebuke of one who had spoken blasphemy.

Nothing more was added. The words seemed to fall like balm on all who heard them. The sobs were hushed, and soon the family retired from the grave leaving their dead with God, who decrees whatever time shall bring to pass.

It was now three o'clock and immediate preparations to return were necessary that we might reach the nearest inn before the night was far advanced. As we drove away we were powerfully impressed with the beauty and grandeur of the surrounding country, and remarked that there was a peculiar fitness between the strong and original character of the man and the region he had chosen for his final home, and long resting place.

North Elba was then, and is now, aside from its great summer hotels, but a plantation in the wilderness, a small hamlet of a hundred souls or so. The little cottage now became historic and a much frequented shrine for hero-worship, stands on an elevated plain, faces the east and overlooks a magnificent prospect of wild grandeur, of rugged mountains and a vast primeval forest, awful in its solitude and silence. Just the country one would say for the heroic soul of John Brown and a proper place to be the receptacle of his ashes.

Wendell Phillips once said that Massachusetts will eventually claim John Brown's remains for interment within her own soil. May it never be! Let them stay beside the great boulder, itself a relic of the ancient glacial age, bearing as it now does on its longest slope, in letters a foot long, the inscription:

JOHN BROWN, Dec. 2nd, 1859,

And where nature's own hand has builded for his lasting monument:

> The great watchtowers of the mountains
> And they lift their heads far into the sky
> And gaze ever upward and around
> To see if the judge of the world come not.

When I got back to Burlington I had been gone just two days. The next day was Saturday, the next Sunday.

How vividly I recall that day, my text, my sermon, my subject. Its example of lowly service, washing his disciples' feet, the symbol of willingness to serve for love's sake. I remarked the appearance of the congregation, many new faces, seldom or never seen there before, and many familiar ones conspicuous by their absence, and in the atmosphere a certain unmistakable indication that things were different. But nothing visible occurred, only a sort of sea-turn had set in and a chilling mist hung on the air.

The next day I learned what had happened. Six of the wealthiest families of my parish had taken an oath and gone over to a neighboring church; others, not a few, who follow in the train of the rich were equally disaffected. On all sides the arrows of public rebuke began to fly. On the street I observed that old friends seeing me coming, suddenly remembered that they had forgotten something and turned back, or, crossing over passed by on the other side. And when the next issue of the Burlington Sentinel appeared, a copperhead sheet—it opened its batteries upon me with a full broadside, and even women stepped in to serve at the guns, and their shots were sharper than the men's. My motives, my life-aims, my principles were made the target of insinuation, misrepresentation, ridicule and abuse. I was called all manner of names. I was an anarchist, a traitor to my country. I was an infidel, a blasphemer, and a vile associate of Garrison and Phillips.

In the course of a day or two there appeared on the street a copy of the *New York Illustrated News*, and oh! What merriment there was, with many a gibe and jeer, in shop and store, wherever men met together, even the pictures it contained: the funeral scenes, the family and the participants in the ceremonies of the occasion, and of course, the officiating clergyman was not left out, but was there with the usual exaggeration of caricature. To more or less of my friends who had up to this time half stood by me, it then seemed no doubt as if my face had been put into the rogues' gallery; that I had not only brought odium upon myself, but shame and confusion of face to them, and to the church of which I was pastor, grievous reproach.

It was indeed a melancholy state of affairs, be it confessed, but it was of a piece with the whole disordered condition of the Country. The times were stormy, they were a vexed and tossing sea, and every body was dizzy.

No one who did not live and move among those eventful times which tried men's souls, certainly no one born since the Civil War can have any the least adequate conception of the then existing political and social condition of the country, and the fierce division of the public mind.

Going to the burial of John Brown I left Burlington a respected and beloved pastor. I returned to find myself in disgrace, an exile in the place of my residence, and little better than a social outcast. Honorable men there were who suggested that it would be a spectacle not for tears, to see me dangling at the end of a rope from the highest tree on the common, swinging and twisting in the wind.

As I come to the conclusion of my story I feel almost ashamed of this personal detail in connection with an instance of moral greatness which properly disposes to silence and meditation.

Let me take my leave be reminding the reader that all advances in justice, in morality, in liberty have been imposed upon, or forced from, society by some noble violence. "Sacrifice is the passion of great souls." That crusade at Harpers Ferry was under God's eye. Virginia, "the mother of presidents," where the blow was struck, was a slave-breeding State, and as such had incorporated licentiousness into a commercial system and prostituted half her women. Brown's enterprise against slavery was not a piece of spite or revenge for the terrible wrongs he and his sons had suffered in Kansas, a plot of ten or twenty years, but the keeping of a vow made to heaven in his early youth.

When a mere lad, seeing a slave boy about his own age, cruelly ill-treated, he writes in his diary: "I swear eternal enmity against slavery." Become a man he is writing letters to his brothers, lamenting the sluggish conscience of the church, and discussing peaceful methods for the abolishment of the barbarous institution. Then again we see him calling his sons together to pledge them, kneeling in prayer, to give their lives to anti-slavery work.

"Born with a hunger for righteousness, his soul was kindled with the purest and most passionate love of liberty, and under the shaping and controlling serenity of this idea, he lived all his life. He pressed all his powers into the spirit and endless pursuit of freedom. This object was the head-waters of his whole career from his youth up," and explains all.

Would we therefore be fair, would we be just, would we judge righteous judgment and measure the moral bulk and stature of this man? We must see with the eye of the spirit that the majesty of his undertaking is not in what he did, that is, in that ill-starred invasion of Virginia, but in the purpose for which he sacrifices his life—in its last analysis, that this great continent might be free!

In the eloquent words of Frederick Douglass [1818-1895] in whose veins mingled the blood of both races, "it stands out in the annals of history with peculiar originality. In its human and divine sympathy crashed through like a bolt from the sky and broke down all suggestions of human prudence.

All down the ages men had been known to die in defense of their own liberty, and for that of their friends, and all the world had applauded such examples. But the example of John Brown is as far as heaven is from earth, above such examples. It is lifted above self, family, friend, race. No chains had bound his ankle. No yoke had galled his neck. It was not for his own freedom, or the freedom of a family, or the freedom of a class that he laid down his life. It was not Caucasian for Caucasian; not white man for white man; not rich man for rich man; but it was Caucasian for Ethiopian, rich man for poor man, white man for black man; the man admitted and respected for the man despised and rejected."

O story of divinest love, of splendid fate! Outside of the New Testament it has no parallel in human history. His was one of those deaths which give life unto the world, which compress into a single hour the purposes of a century. His name shall never perish out of the memory and the wonder of men.

"He lived, he died to be forever known
And make each age to come his own."

PRAYER

Almighty and most merciful God! We lift our souls unto thee, and bow our hearts to the unutterable emotions of this hour. O Lord thus alone art our sufficient help. Open thou our lips and our mouth shall show forth thy praise. Thou art speaking unto us, as in these grand and solemn scenes of nature, so in the great and solemn circumstances which have brought us together here. Our souls are filled with awe, and are subdued to silence, as we think of that great, heroic, reverential soul, whose mortal remains we are now to commit to the grave, dust to dust, while his spirit dwells with God who gave it, and his memory is enshrined in every pure and loving heart.

At his open grave, as standing by the altar of the Christ, the divinest friend and Saviour of man, may we consecrate ourselves anew to the work of Truth, Righteousness and Love, forevermore to sympathize with the outcast and the oppressed, with the humble and the least of our suffering fellow-men.

We pray for these afflicted ones—this sadly bereaved and mourning family. O God, hear our prayers. We pray for the widow and for the fatherless. O Lord, put underneath them thy everlasting arm and grant them the richest consolation of thy Holy Spirit.

But, Father in heaven, in imitation of the self-forgetfulness and self-sacrifice of this great departed, our saint and hero—putting aside all personal anguish and all private grief, we supplicate in this great hour thy special blessing upon those helpless and despised ones, the poor enslaved for whom our brother laid down his life. O God, cause the oppressed to go free, break every yoke, and bring down the pride and prejudice that dare lift themselves up. Hasten on the day when no more wrong or injustice shall be done on the earth; when all men shall love one another without dissimulation, with true brotherly love, and love thou with pure hearts fervently, who art the God and Father of all mankind, and with whom there is no respect of persons, the all just and merciful, and shall do thy will with all their souls and with all their strength. Which we ask in the name and as the disciple of Jesus Christ.

Amen.

Excerpt from the *Fall River Daily Herald*, February 9, 1904:

OBITUARY.
Joshua Young.

Rev. Joshua Young, formerly pastor of the Unitarian church in this city, is dead at Groton, Mass. He was 81 years old at the time of his death.

It was Dr. Young who preached at the funeral of John Brown when the body was brought from Harpers Ferry after the execution to the Adirondacks. At that time great difficulty was experienced in getting a clergyman to officiate at the burial, but Dr. Young, who was then preaching at Burlington, Vt. volunteered. For this action he was greatly criticized by the pro-slavery element in his parish and he resigned in indignation. A few years ago he delivered an address at the grave of John Brown, the occasion being an anniversary.

Dr. Young was pastor of the Unitarian church in this

city for seven years, beginning in 1869. He was greatly respected by people of all denominations while here. He resigned on account of increasing deafness and went to a smaller parish in Groton, Mass, where he has preached for more than a quarter century. He always retained pleasant relations with his old parishioners in this city and was on many occasions called to officiate at funerals here, the last being the funeral of Mrs. Dr. Foster Hooper [*née Nancy L. Wood*] four years ago.

Those who knew him while he was located in this city will recall pleasant memories of his genial presence and fine thought. As his deafness increased he was shut out to some extent from the outer world and his sermons became more and more spiritual. He was a student of specialized philosophy and while he represented the more conservative phase of Unitarianism he would never consent to the endorsement of any creed or articles of faith. He believed in absolute soul liberty.

The following three personal letters were written by two of John Brown's daughters to the Rev. Joshua Young. They are contained in an archive of Young family material held in the Charlton Library of Fall River History at the Fall River Historical Society; they are published here for the first time.

Mrs. Samuel Adams, née Annie Brown (1843-1926) to Reverend Joshua Young, March 17, 1899. Wove paper, ruled; two sheets, single fold, embossed "National," unidentified manufacturer.

> Petrolia Humboldt Co[*unty*] Cal[*ifornia*]
> May 19th 1897
> Rev. Joshua Young
> Groton, Mass[*achusetts*]
>
> My Dear Friend
> I received your most kind letter of May 3rd yesterday

Humboldt Co.
Petrolia, Cal. May 19th 1897,

Rev, Joshua Young
Groton, Mass,

            My Dear Friend
                I recieved your
most kind letter of May 3rd
Yesterday with the enclosed
$10.00 Please accept my
heartfelt thanks for your
great kindness to me, I shall
hold you in grateful remembrance as long as I live,
I will remember you as the
Young minister who, with
Wendell Phillipps, and
Mr. J. M. McKim of Phila, Pa,
officiated at my fathers
funeral,

57. Letter from John Brown's daughter, Annie (Brown) Adams, to Rev. Joshua Young, May 19, 1897: "What a wonderful progress the negro race have made…."

with the enclosed $10.00. Please accept my heartfelt thanks for your great kindness to me. I shall hold you in grateful remembrance as long as I live. I will remember you as the young minister who, with Wendall Phillipps [*Wendell Phillips (1811-1884), abolitionist, attorney, and orator*] and Mr. J. M. McKim [*James Miller McKim (1810-1874) Presbyterian minister and abolitionist who accompanied the body of John Brown to New York*] of Phila[*delphia*], P[*ennsylvania*] officiated at my father's funeral. How few of us who were there are now left.

It seems to me that I have lived two lives—one before and one since that event. What a wonderful progress the negro race have made since their freedom and that in less than half a century, too. They put our boasted civilization to shame more and more every year. If they do not stand on the rock, of tobacco and intemperance, where the white race is so rapidly becoming shipwrecked, they will outstrip us in a few generations. I think the war of races will soon cease, and it will be "a survival of the fittest" in the next century.

If you will write to the *Hudson Independent*, a paper published at Hudson, Ohio, where father and grandfather [*Owen Brown (1771-1856)*] once lived, and procure copies of that paper, containing the recollections of a "Pioneer By Lora Case" that is now running as a serial in that paper, you will get some very interesting pieces for your scrapbook, something new and decidedly original. [*She is referring to "Hudson of Long Ago: Progress of Hudson during the past century, personal reminiscences of an aged pioneer" written by Lora Case (1811-1897), a childhood friend of John Brown.*]

The old man sends them to me. I received a very interesting letter from him a short-time since. He has a letter written to him, by my father, on Dec[*ember*] 2nd 1859, which he publishes in these papers (for I think the first-time.) It is one of his best; Do not fail to procure it.

May our Heavenly Father abundantly bless you and all the good friends, who have been so kind to me in my misfortune and reward you here and hereafter.

With best wishes for you and yours I am most cordially yours
Annie Brown Adams

P.S. If you have not already read it, you will find a great deal that is new and interesting in "John Brown and his Men," a book by Col. Richard J. Hinton [*Richard Josiah Hinton (1830-1910)*], published by the Funk and Wagnalls Co. New York.

A. B. A.

Mrs. Samuel Adams, née Annie Brown (1843-1926) to Reverend Joshua Young, March 9, 1899. Wove paper; two sheets, single fold; Imperial Irish Linen watermark of Raynor & Perkins, New York, New, York; with holograph envelope; wove paper, unidentified manufacturer.

Petrolia, Humboldt Co. Cali[*fornia*].
March 5th 1899

Rev. Joshua Young
Groton, Mass[*achusetts*]

My Dear Friend
I received the copy of the *Boston Globe* you so kindly sent me this morning. Thanks for the courtesy. Please allow me even at this late date, to offer my best wishes for future happiness and blessings, to you and your wife. May you continue to be one another's best Valentines for years to come. [*She is referring to Rev. & Mrs. Joshua Young's Golden Wedding Anniversary, celebrated on February 11, 1899.*]

It is allowed to some to outlive their earthly trials and rest for a while, before taking their departure to eternal rest. If indeed perfect rest ever comes to mortals, even in the hereafter.

Petrolia, Humboldt Co. Cala.
March 5th 1899,

Rev, Joshua Young,
Groton, Mass,
My Dear Friend
I recieved the
copy of the ~~Boston Globe~~ you so
kindly sent me this morning.
Thanks for the courtesy.
Please allow me even at this
late date, to offer my best-wishes
for future happiness and blessings,
to you and your wife, May you
continue to be one another's best
Valentines for years to come,
It is allowed to some to outlive

58. Letter from John Brown's daughter, Annie (Brown) Adams, to Rev. Joshua Young, March 5, 1899: "I shall not forget your kindness in our time of deep affliction...."

We think our gratitude to you, when we enjoy the warmth and comfort of the little stove purchased with the money so kindly sent us by you.

We have had unusually cold weather a part of this winter, two snow storms and a good deal of real freezing weather, and abundance of rain and a goodly amount of sunshine mixed, so we have no occasion for complaining like the people in other parts of this state.

In the latter part of last December [*December 27, 1898*] my Uncle Adair of Osawatomie, Kansas, died. [*Reverend Samuel Lyle Adair (1811-1898), husband of John Brown's half-sister, née Florilla Brown (1816-1865)*]. My Aunt Martha L. Davis [*Mrs. Stephen Callendar Davis, née Martha Lucretia Brown, half-sister of John Brown*] of Saint Johns, Michigan, my father's youngest sister and the last surviving member of Grandfather's [*Owen Brown (1771-1856)*] sixteen children, was staying at her son's [*Dwight L. Davis (1856-1932)*] at Kansas City Mo [*Missouri*], waiting for the weather to moderate so she could go on to Osawatomie to visit him, when she received a telegram to come immediately to attend his funeral. She sent the obituary notice which I enclose, for you to read, thinking it might interest you to read of another who had tried to do his duty, regardless of consequences. Please return it to me as it is the only copy of it that I have.

Believe me that as long as memory lasts, that I shall not forget your kindness in our time of deep affliction, when you officiated at my (then considered outlaw,) father's funeral, nor your efficient aid when misfortune recently overtook us.

With love and best wishes to your family. May Our Heavenly Father bless and abundantly reward you.

Most Sincerely Yours

Annie Brown Adams

⁕

Mrs. Henry Thompson, née Ruth Brown (1843-1926) to Reverend Joshua Young, March 17, 1899. Wove paper; one sheet, single fold; unidentified manufacturer.

Pasadena California
March 17- 1899

Rev. Dr. Young

My Dear Friend of long ago.

In the *Christian Advocate* of March 9th I read an article, headed "Reproach changed to honor"*. It said you had just celebrated the fiftieth anniversary of your ordination, and the twenty fifth of your pastorate of the first parish church. When I read this, this morning, I could not resist the desire to write and tell you that in all these years since you attended my dear father's funeral, you are not forgotten. The prayer you made before going to the grave, and what you said after the dear father was lowered into the grave made my heart go out to you in deepest gratitude. Your prayer, was so comforting to my crushed and lonely heart, by what seemed to me then, the taking away from me the love of my precious father. He seemed lost to me. O, have I prayed to God, to spare his dear life. But, I was wrong. He was not lost. I am thankful that I never felt bitter towards those who took his life—"They knew not what they did"—Now after so many years, I have heard of you who dared to preach and pray for John Brown, who was so despised by those (who thought they were Christians) and you who was treated so unjustly that you resigned the pastorate of your church. I felt that you were cruelly treated and felt hurt for you.

You gave a lecture on John Brown, at Wadhams Falls [*New York*] which I attended. Then you sent me a pamphlet of a sermon or lecture you gave after. I was so pleased with it, that I sent it to my brother John Jr. [*John*

59. Letter from John Brown's daughter, Ruth (Brown) Thompson, to Rev. Joshua Young, March 17, 1899: "you who dared to preach and pray for John Brown."

Brown Jr. (1821-1895)] Wish I had it here to put in my big scrapbook of articles written about father.

Dear Mr. Young, do not think I am presuming to write to you, for I love your memory, and would be delighted to hear from you. Should be more than glad to see you in our humble but happy home in Pasadena. Mr. Thompson [*her husband, Henry Thompson (1822-1911)]* is quite well. He is eighty years old. Two of our married daughters live here [*Mrs. Francis Newton Towne, née Ella J. Thompson (1856-1948), and Mrs. John Lamport Simmons, née Grace Ruth Thompson (1858-1921)].* Our youngest daughter [*Mary E. Thompson (1872-1939)]* teaches in the sixth grade in the Garfield School [*James A. Garfield Elementary School]* here. I met Ms. Garfield at a reception last week. [*She is referring to the widow of President James Abram Garfield, née Lucretia Rudolph (1832-1918), who maintained a winter residence in Pasadena, California.*]

Rev. Dr. Conger [*Eugene L. Conger (1851-1914)],* of the Universalist church [*Throop Unitarian Universalist Church]* in Pasadena, is a dear friend of mine. We meet a good many of God's true men and women here. Pasadena is about as near Heaven as I ever expect to get in this life. With kind loving remembrance I am yours gratefully

Ruth Brown Thompson
P.O. Box 27 Pasadena Los Angeles
Co[*unty*] California

Here are some orange blossoms. Wish they could reach you in their snowy waxen beauty.

[*The article she referred to appeared under the heading "At Home and Abroad" in the* Christian Advocate, *Vol. 74, March 9, 1899: "Reproach Changed to Honor—Dr. Young, of Groton, Mass., has just celebrated the fiftieth anniversary of his ordination and the twenty-fifth of his pastorate of the first parish church. When John Brown was buried alongside of the great stone at Elba, in the Adirondacks, Dr. Young was then pastor of Burlington, within easy access of Elba. Wendell Phillips, who was an orthodox Congregationalist, asked him to officiate after several other ministers had declined. William Lloyd Garrison, who was not orthodox, was to speak at some length. As a result of this Dr. Young was ostracized, which finally resulted in resigning his charge. The* Worcester Spy, *which gives the facts, says time has changed to honor and distinction what was once treated as a reproach."*]

Bibliography

Published Sources:

Adams, George. *Fall River Directory for 1855*. Fall River, Massachusetts: Robert Adams, 1855.

Adams, James Truslow. *The March of Democracy: A History of the United States*. New York, New York: Scribner's Sons, 1932.

Chace, Elizabeth Buffum. *Anti-Slavery Reminiscences*. Central Falls, Rhode Island: E.L. Freeman & Son, State Printer, 1891.

Geoffrey, Theodate, (nom de plume of Dorothy Wayman Godfrey). *Suckanasset: A History of Falmouth, Massachusetts 1661-1930*. Falmouth, Massachusett: Falmouth Publishing Company, 1930.

Hutchinson Family Singers. *The Hutchinson Family's Book of Words*. New York, New York: Godwin & Company, 1851.

Lovell, Malcolm Read. *Two Quaker Sister: From the Original Diaries of Elizabeth Buffum Chace and Lucy Buffum Lovell*. New York, New York: Liveright Publishing Corporation, 1937.

Munro, Wilfred Harold. *The History of the Town of Bristol, R.I.: The Story of the Mount Hope Lands*. Providence, Rhode Island: J.A. & R.A. Reid, 1880.

Pierce, Palo Alto. *A History of the Town Freetown, Massachusetts*. Fall River, Massachusetts: J. H. Franklin & Company, 1902.

Siebert, Prof. Wilbur Henry. *The Underground Railroad from Slavery to Freedom*. London, England: The MacMillan & Company Ltd., 1898.

Stowe, Harriet Beecher Stowe. *Uncle Tom's Cabin*. Boston, Massachusetts: John P. Blewett & Company, 1852.

The Southern Workman: Vol. XXXV, No. 5, May, 1906. Hampton, Virginia: Hampton Normal and Agricultural Institute.

Weeden, William Babcock. *Early Rhode Island: A Social History of the People*. New York, New York: The Grafton Press, 1910.

Unpublished Sources:

Gardner, Orrin Augustus. "Swansea: Its History and Story." Presented to the Fall River Historical Society, March 31, 1930.
Hawes, Oliver Snow. "The Story of the Stone House." Presented to the Fall River Historical Society, November 30, 1936.
Mosher, Flora E. Mosher. "The Toll House and the East End." Presented to the Fall River Historical Society, October 20, 1933.

Ephemera:

Get Off the Track!. Boston, Massachusetts: Henry Prentiss, Publishers, 1844.
John Brown Song. Philadelphia, Pennsylania: Johnson Song Publishers, Stationers, and Printers, 1861.

Newspapers:

Christian Advocate
Fall River All Sorts and Tiverton Advertiser
Fall River News
Hudson Independent
Tea Party Gazette
The Fall River Monitor

Papers and Pamphlets:

Address of the Ladies Anti-Slavery Society of Fall River to the Christian Women of Fall River. Fall River, Massachusetts: Ladies Anti-Slavery Society of Fall River, circa 1840.
Declaration of Sentiments of the American Anti-Slavery Convention. Philadelphia, Pennsylvania: American Anti-Slavery Society, December 6, 1833.
Haughwout, Reverend Peter Britton. *An Address Suggested by the Times.* Fall River, Massachusetts: Almy & Milne, Publishers, 1861.
Siebert, Prof. Wilbur Henry. *The Underground Railroad in Massachusetts.* Worcester, Massachusetts: American Antiquarian Society, Vol.45; American Antiquarian Society, 1935.
Westall, Reverend John. *In Memoriam.* Fall River, Massachusetts: Almy, Milne & Company, 1865.

ABOUT THE FALL RIVER HISTORICAL SOCIETY

Incorporated in 1921, Fall River Historical Society (FRHS), a public charity, is the oldest cultural institution in the city that is dedicated to collecting and exhibiting artifacts and archival material relative to the history and multi-cultural people of Fall River. We serve the public through guided tours, exhibitions, educational programs, publications, and cultural events, and frequently partner with the city and other non-profit organizations in presenting events for the benefit of the community. The FRHS is recognized in the Greater Fall River area as a leading provider of innovative historical and cultural programming.

The FRHS was founded in 1921 by a group of individuals intent on preserving the history of Fall River, once an important textile center with the distinction of being the world's largest producer of cotton cloth. Since its incorporation, the organization has been actively acquiring material pertaining to the city's history and has amassed a vast collection, the majority of which is accompanied by detailed provenance.

A tragic set-back occurred on the evening of February 2, 1928, when a devastating conflagration destroyed a large section of the Fall River business district. Among the victims, and situated almost in the center of the burned out area, was the supposedly fire-proof Buffington Building, which housed the office and exhibition room of the FRHS. The entire collection was lost, except for a selection of important items stored in a safe, which survived the inferno unscathed. Undaunted, the organization immediately resumed gathering material, thereby forming the nucleus of the collection as it exists today.

The diverse collections of the FRHS continue to grow in all categories, and include: Americana; Costumes and Accessories; Decorative Arts; Ephemera; Fall River Textile Industry; Furniture; Local History; Manuscripts; Maritime; Paintings, Drawings, and Sculpture,

19th Century; Paintings, Drawings, and Sculpture, 20th Century and Contemporary; and Photographs. Items from our collections have been loaned for exhibition at institutions nationwide.

The vast majority of the FRHS's holdings are acquired by gift. In addition, we seek out and purchase items of historical importance through the generosity of private donors and donations made to our Acquisition Fund.

The FRHS has been collecting archival and library material pertaining to Fall River history since its incorporation, with examples dating from the late-seventeenth to the mid-twentieth century; the holdings, which are ever-growing, constitute the largest collection of its type extant in the city. In 2009, the library and archive was designated The Charlton Library of Fall River History in recognition of the Ida S. Charlton Charity Fund, which sponsored the expansion and refitting of the facility and the conservation of a portion of the Society's holdings. The Fund made an additional contribution in 2012, allowing further expansion and, in 2016, a generous grant from the Earle P. Charlton Jr. Charity Fund made advanced development possible.

The library, which is non-circulating, houses an important research collection of books, pamphlets, periodicals, and reference materials. Published material includes biographies, *Fall River City Directories*, local authors, genealogy, family histories, memoirs, municipal documents, periodicals, and regional histories pertinent to the city of Fall River, as well as city, county, economic, ethnic, industrial, maritime, military, Native American, political, and social histories. Select baptismal, business, church, and probate records are available, as are a large number of unpublished papers and manuscripts. Materials are added to the library on a regular basis.

Holdings include a microfilm collection containing in excess of 100,000 issues of 19th and 20th century Fall River newspapers, with the earliest dating to 1858, as well as scrapbooks compiled by private individuals and organizations. The Society's manuscript collection contains thousands of documents, including family and personal papers, corporate and legal documents, business records, church records, diaries, and journals. Also available is the most extensive collection of Fall River textile mill records and manuscripts in existence.

The photograph collection contains thousands of examples, and is widely recognized as the most comprehensive assemblage of its type pertaining to Fall River. With images dating from the dawn of photography to the mid-20th century, the collection documents the changing landscape of the city's public and private spaces, its cultural development, and the faces of its inhabitants.

The FRHS is recognized, world-wide, as the central repository for material pertaining to the infamous 1892 Borden Murder Case and the life of Lizzie Andrew Borden (1860-1827), who was tried and acquitted for that heinous crime. The Borden collections, which are unsurpassed, include original trial exhibits, photographs, and the most significant primary source material extant.

The FRHS operates Fall River Historical Society Press, dedicated to publishing works on a wide range of historical topics, with all proceeds benefiting the organization.

For more information about Fall River Historical Society, visit our website at fallriverhistorical.org, or contact us at 508-679-1071.

ACKNOWLEDGMENTS

The Fall River Historical Society is deeply indebted to Nancy A. Teasdale, who has voluntarily spent untold hours transcribing the original manuscript of this and numerous other papers that were presented at society meetings in decades past. Her diligent perseverance, without which the *Discourses on History* series would not be possible, is hereby gratefully acknowledged.

Special thanks to the following for their research and assistance in the preparation of this volume:

Caroline H. Aubin
Constance C. Mendes
David J. Roseberry
Cynthia Tobojka
Swan Imaging:
    Bill Crombie
    Susan Crombie

INDEX

by Stefani Koorey, PhD

Entries are arranged in word-by-word order, using the *Chicago Manual of Style, 16th Edition*. References to page numbers for illustrations are indicated by numerals in bold type.

All females are listed by their last known surname, followed in parentheses by maiden name, with cross-references provided from maiden name for ease of location. In places where maiden surnames are unknown, first names are provided. All placenames, including streets, companies, churches, and schools, are located in Fall River, Massachusetts, unless specifically noted. All anti-slavery societies are designated by their location, regardless of whether they are located in Fall River, MA.

A

Abolitionism, xvii, xviii, 13, 15
Adair, Mrs. Archibald Richard, III, (formerly, Mrs. George Walter Clapp; Mrs. Jacob Harding; Mrs. William P. Thompson; née Mary Elizabeth Brown), 103
Adair, Mrs. Samuel Lyle, (née Florilla Brown), 114
Adair, Reverend Samuel Lyle, 114
Adams, Edward Stowe, xxi, **xvi**, xvii–xix, **68**
Adams, Mrs. Edward Stowe [1], (née Eva J. Palmer), xix
Adams, Mrs. Edward Stowe [2], (née Carrie Maria Smith), xix
Adams, James Truslow, 31, 40
Adams, John, 19
Adams, Robert, xvii, 19, 23, 24, 25, 26, 29, 43, 61, 77
Adams, Mrs. Robert, (née Lydia Ann Stowe), xvii–xviii, 12, 54, 57, **58**, 70
Adams, Mrs. Samuel, (née Annie Brown) letter to Reverend Joshua Young, 109–112, **110**, 112–114, **113**
Adams Bookstore, xvii
Aldrich, Dr. James Mott, **42**, 43
Almy, Hannah T. *See* Almy, Mrs. Thomas
Almy, Mrs. Thomas, (née Hannah T. Almy), 12
American Antiquarian Society, 21

American Missionary Society, 60
Andrew, Governor John Albion, 95–96
Anti-Fugitive Slave Law Society, 35
Anti-Slavery Reminiscences, 16, 22–23
anti-slavery societies, 7, 9, 10, 36, 50
Anti-Slavery Society (R.I.), 50
Archer, Dr. Jason Hawes, 35
Armstrong, General Samuel Chapman, 60

B

Bailey, Frederick Augustus Washington. *See* Douglass, Frederick
Baker, Frank (slave), 59
Baptist Meeting House, 13
Bass, Willliam, 61
Battelle, Hezekiah letter from, 10
Baumfree, Isabella 'Bell.' *See* Truth, Sojourner
Beecher, Harriet Elizabeth. *See* Stowe, Harriet Beecher
Beers, Charles, 12
Beers, Sarah Garfield. *See* Hall, Mrs. John V.
Bellows, Mrs. Dr. Howard Perry, 50, 53
Berean Temple, 12
Bigelow, Lucius Henry, 100, 103
Blaisdell, Josiah Coleman, 43
Borden, Holder, 10

Borden, Nathaniel Briggs, 15, 17, 24, 32, 33, 36, 43
  home of (station on the Underground Railroad), **18**
  letter to, 10, 40
Borden, Mrs. Nathaniel Briggs, (née Sarah Gould Buffum), 8, 23, 29
Boston, MA
  Abolitionism in, 27
Boston Advertiser, 35
Boston Female Anti-Slavery Society, 9
Boston Globe, 112
Bowen, Abraham, 11, 29, 31
  home of (station on the Underground Railroad), **32**
Bowen, Joseph Abraham, **52**
Bradford, Governor William, 1
Brewster, Martha Evelyn. *See* Brown, Mrs. Oliver
Bristol, R.I.
  slave trade in, 1–2
Bristol County Anti-Slavery Society (MA), 11
Bronson, Reverend Asa, 32, **33**
Brown, Annie. *See* Adams, Mrs. Samuel
Brown, Ellen. *See* Fablinger, Mrs. James Beatty
Brown, Florilla. *See* Adair, Mrs. Samuel Lyle
Brown, John, 24, 43–45, **44**, 53, 92, 93, 108, 111, 115, 117
  "The Funeral of John Brown," 93–108
  grave marker of, 104
Brown, John, Jr., 115, 117
Brown, Captain John, 103
Brown, Mrs. John, (née Mary Ann Day), 96, 97, 98, 99, 102, 103
Brown, Martha Lucretia. *See* Davis, Mrs. Stephen Callendar
Brown, Mary Elizabeth. *See* Adair, Mrs. Archibald Richard, III
Brown, Oliver, 93, 94
Brown, Mrs. Oliver, (née Martha Evelyn Brewster), 103
Brown, Owen, 111, 114
Brown, Peter, 99
Brown, Mrs. Salmon. *See* Brown, Mrs. Watson
Brown, Watson, 94–95, 103
Brown, Mrs. Watson, (née Isabella Thompson), 103
Brown University, xviii, 1
Buchanan, President James, 74
Buffington, Mrs. Edward, (née Sarah Ann Hathaway), 12
Buffinton, Benjamin, **52**
Buffinton, Francis, 64
Buffinton, Nathan, 17
Buffinton, Oliver, 64
Buffinton, Mrs. Oliver, (née Elizabeth Mason Reynolds), 64
Buffum, Arnold, 4, **4**, 8, 11

Buffum, Elizabeth. *See* Chace, Mrs. William Buffington
Buffum, Louisa. *See* Hawes, Mrs. William Mowry
Buffum, Lucy. *See* Lovell, Mrs. Reverend Nehemiah Gorham
Buffum, Sarah Gould. *See* Borden, Mrs. Nathaniel Briggs
Burleigh, Charles Calistus, 50
Burns, Anthony (fugitive slave), 26, **27**, 40, 88, 99
Burnside, General Ambrose, 66
Butler, General Benjamin Franklin, 59, 60
Butler Contraband School, 60
Byfield, Colonel Nathaniel, 83

C
Canedy, Anne Chaloner Graves, 28, 66, 70, **71**, 72–73, 75
  letter from, 70, 72–73
Canedy, Betsey Leonard, 28, 66, 69–70
Canedy, Mary Bridge. *See* Slade, Mrs. Albion King
Canedy, William Barnabas, 66
  home of (station on the Underground Railroad), 19, **22**
Canedy, Mrs. William Barnabas, (née Susan Hughes Luther), 66
Case, Lora, 111
Central Congregational Church, 60
Chace, Adelia Bartlett, 26
Chace, Arnold Buffum, 26
Chace, Edward Gould, 26
Chace, Elizabeth Buffum "Lillie." *See* Wyman, Mrs. John Crawford
Chace, George Arnold, 26
Chace, John Gould, 26
Chace, Mary Elizabeth. *See* Chaney, Mrs. Horace Rundlett; Tolman, Mrs. James Pike
Chace, Oliver, 26
Chace, Samuel Buffington, 26
Chace, Samuel Oliver, 26
Chace, Susan Elizabeth, 26
Chace, William Buffington, 16
  home of (station on the Underground Railroad), **23**
Chace, Mrs. William Buffington, (née Elizabeth Buffum), 8, **14**, 15, 16, 17, 22–23, 26, 31, 88
Chaney, Mrs. Horace Rundlett, (née Mary Elizabeth Chace), 26
Charlton Library of Fall River History, xxi, 93, 109
Cheever, Reverend Dr. George Barrrell, 95
Cheney, Mrs. Seth Wells, (née Ednah Dow Littlehale), 95
Choate, Rufus, 40
Christian Advocate, 115, 117
Christian Women of Fall River, 29

Church of the Ascension, 31
Church of the Puritans (N.Y.), 95
Clapp, Mrs. George Walter, (née Mary
  Elizabeth Brown). *See* Adair, Mrs. Archibald
  Richard, III
Clarke, Dr. Henry Bradford, 50, 52
Clarke, Mrs. Dr. Henry Bradford, (née Martha
  C. Little), 52
Clarke, Dr. John Lewis, 50
Clarke, Mary Anna. *See* Bellows, Mrs. Dr.
  Howard Perry
Clarke, Dr. Peleg, 50
Clay, Henry, 13
Coburn, Mary. *See* Young, Mrs. Aaron
Coffin, Lucretia. *See* Mott, Mrs. John
Columbian Hall, 12
Commander, Edmund, **62–63**
Congdon, Eunice Hathaway, 54, **56**, 57, 59,
  60–61, 62–63, 64, 65
Conger, Reverend Dr. Eugune L., 117
Crank, Catherine C. *See* Simpson, Mrs. Elisha
Curry, James (fugitive slave), 22

D
Davis, Dwight L., 114
Davis, Jefferson, 75
Davis, Hon. Dr. Robert Thompson, **42**, 43
Davis, Mrs. Hon. Dr. Robert Thompson, (née
  Sarah Congdon Wilbur), 12
Davis, Mrs. Stephen Callendar, (née Martha
  Lucretia Brown), 114
Day, Mary Ann. *See* Brown, Mrs. John
*The Declaration of Sentiments of the American
  Anti-Slavery Convention*, 5–8
Democratic Party, 13
DeWolfe, Captain James, 1–2, 83
Diman, Jeremiah, 83
Dixon, George Emerson, 60, 65
Dixon, Mrs. George Emerson. *See* Congdon,
  Eunice Hathaway
Douglass, Frederick, xviii, 50, 54, 77, **79**,
  106–107

E
*Early Rhode Island: A Social History of the
  People*, 16
Emancipation Proclamation, 54, 59
Emerson, Ralph Waldo, 40, 96
Episcopal Church Pearl Street Chapel, 11
Everett, His Excellency Edward, 15

F
Fablinger, Mrs. James Beatty, (née Ellen
  Brown), 103
Fall River, MA, *73*
  Adams Bookstore, xvii
  Athenaeum, 46
  Baptist Meeting House, 13
  Berean Temple, 12

(Fall River, MA, cont.)
  Central Congregational Church, 60
  Charlton Library of Fall River History, xxi,
    93, 109
  Christian Women of Fall River, 29
  Church of the Ascension, 31
  Episcopal Church Pearl Street Chapel, 11
  Fall River, 1839, **13**
  Fall River Anti-Slavery Sewing Circle, 12
  Fall River Anti-Slavery Society, 10, 11, 13,
    15, 32
  Fall River Female Anti-Slavery Society, 10,
    11, 12, 13, 29, 31, 33, 36
  Fall River High School, xviii
  Fall River Historical Society, xxi, xvii, 1, 2,
    19, 93, 109
    false bookcase in the, 18–19
    as station on the Underground
      Railroad, 17
  Fall River Temperance Society, 13
  Fall River Women's Union, xviii
  Fireman's Hall, 11
  First Baptist Church, 43, 54, 60
  First Baptist Meeting House, 9, 11, 33
  First Congregational Church, xxi, 11, 34,
    35
  Great Fire of 1843, 12, **12**, 31
  Methodist Chapel, 13
  Quaker Meeting House, 60, **64**
  stations on the Underground Railroad, 17,
    18, 19, **21**, **22**, 26, **32**
  Stone Church, 60
  Town Hall and Market Building, 36, 51
  Town House, 29
  Underground Railroad and, 17–18, 19, 21,
    24, 26
  Unitarian Society, 10
  Young Men's Republican Club of Fall
    River, **52**
The Fall River All Sorts and Tiverton Advertiser,
  11, 31
"Fall River As It Was and As It Is," 45, 47–50
Fall River Herald News, xxi
The Fall River Monitor, 10, 12, 13, 32, 33, 34,
  35, 36
Fall River News, 35, 76
Featherstonhaugh, Dr. Thomas, 93
Fields, Viney A., 64
Fireman's Hall, 11
First African Church (Danville, VA), 60
First Baptist Church, 43, 54, 60
First Baptist Church (Boston, MA), 96
First Baptist Meeting House, 9, 11, 33
First Congregational Church, xxi, 11, 34, 35
First Parish Unitarian Church (Groton, MA),
  88, 91, 108
Fiske, Anna Robinson. *See* Harding, Mrs. Harry
  Theodore
Fiske, George Robinson, 52, 53

Fiske, Dr. Isaac, 43, 50
Fletcher, George F., 51
Fletcher, Margaret, 51
Ford, Squire James, 33, **34**, 65, **68**, 70
Fort Spinola, 70
Fort Sumter, fall of, 59
Fowler, Reverend Orin, 34, 35, **35**
Frederick Douglass Memorial and Historical
     Society of New Bedford, 77
Free Soil Convention, 35
Freedmen's Bureau, 54
Freeman's Purchase, 81
Freemont, John Charles, 52
French, Richard Cornell, 29
French, Stephen Leonard, 29
Friends Association (Philadelphia, PA), 57
Fugitive Slave Act of 1850, 17, 27, 34, 35, 36, 43,
     84, 88, 99
Fuller, J. G., 29
"The Funeral of John Brown," 92, 93–108

G
Gardner, Orrin Augustus, 2–3
Garfield, Mrs. President James Abram, (née
     Lucretia Randolph), 117
Garrison, William Lloyd, 8, 9, 15, 32, 36, 50,
     51–52, 54, 77, 105, 118
"Get Off the Track," 37–39, **38**
Gifford, Benjamin, 3
Godfrey, Dorothy Wayman. *See* Goeffrey,
     Theodate
Goeffrey, Theodate, 3
Goss, Mary Ann. *See* Wilder, Mrs. Dr. Daniel
Green, Dinah, 75
Grimké, Angelina Emily, 50
Grimké, Sarah Moore, 50

H
Haffenreffer, Rudolf Frederick, 1
Hall, Captain E.P., 93
Hall, Mrs. John V., (née Susan Garfield Beers),
     12
Hampton Institute. *See* Hampton University
Hampton Normal & Agricultural Institute. *See*
     Hampton University
Hampton University, 65, 82
Harding, Mrs. Harry Theodore, (née Anna
     Robinson Fiske), 50
Harding, Mrs. Jacob, (née Mary Elizabeth
     Brown). *See* Adair, Mrs. Archibald Richard,
     III
Harpers Ferry (West Virginia), 92, 93, 94, 95,
     96, 99, 102, 103, 106, 108
Harper's Weekly
     sketch of "Freed Negros," **67**
Harris, Sarah D., 12
Hathaway, Jacob, Sr., 83
Hathaway, Sarah Ann. *See* Buffington, Mrs.
     Edward

Haughwout, Reverend Peter Britton, **53**, 54
Hawes, Oliver Snow, 17
Hawes, William Mowry, 52, 52
Hawes, Mrs. William Mowry, (née Louisa
     Buffum), 17, **20**
Hawkins, William Henry
     letter from, 10
Henry, Mayor Alexander, 97
Hill, Friend William, 17, 18, **19**, 20, 21
Hinton, Colonel Richard J., 112
The History of the Town of Bristol, R.I., 83
History of Freetown, 82
A History of the Town Freetown, Massachusetts
     2
Hoge, Matilda. *See* Turner, Mrs. William
Holmes, Charles Jarvis, **52**
Home for the Aged, xviii
Hooper, Dr. Foster, **42**, 43
Hooper, Mrs. Dr. Foster, (née Nancy L. Wood),
     109
Hudson Independent, 111
Hugo, Victor, 96
Hunt, Thomas, 81
Hutchinson, Abby Jermima. *See* Patton, Mrs.
     Ludlow
Hutchinson, Adoniram Judson, 36
Hutchinson, Asa Burnham, 36
Hutchinson, Jesse, 36
Hutchinson, John Wallace, 36
Hutchinson Family Singers, 36, **37**
The Hutchinson Family's Book of Words, 37

J
Jameson, Thorndike Cleaves, 72
"John Brown Song," 43, 45
Jones, Sarah R., 60

K
Kagi, John Henry, 93
King Philip Museum, R.I., 1
King Philip's War, 81

L
Lapham, Louis, 43
Lea, Thomas T., 17
Leary, Lewis Sheridan, 93
Leeman, William Henry, 93
Leland, Dr. Phineas Washington, 43, **46**
     poem by, 45, 47–50
Lewis, John, 75
Libby, Dr. Orin, 93
The Liberator, 8, **9**, 15
Lincoln, President Abraham, 37, 43, 52, 53, 57,
     69–70, 77, 78
Lindsey, James T., 31
Lindsey, Mrs. James T., (née Abby Jane Terry),
     29, 31
Lindsey, Joseph Ferdinand, 65

Little, Martha C. *See* Clarke, Mrs. Dr. Henry Bradford
Littlehale, Ednah Dow. *See* Cheney, Mrs. Seth Wells
Locofoco Party (radical wing of Democratic Party), 13
Longfellow, Henry Wadsworth, 40
Lovell, Malcolm Read, 8
Lovell, Mrs. Reverend Nehemiah Gorham, (née Lucy Buffum), 8, **30**, 31
Lovell, William Buffum, 8
Lowell, James Russell, 40
Luther, Susan Hughes. *See* Canedy, Mrs. William Barnabas

M

McCellan, Katherine Elizabeth, 93
McKim, Reverend James Miller, 98, 103, 111
Mallory, Colonel Charles King, 59
Mallory, Shepard (slave), 59
Manning, Reverend Jacob Merrill, 96
March of Democracy: A History of the United States, 31
Massachusetts Anti-Slavery Society, 4, 77
Massachusetts State Normal School (Lexington, MA), xviii
May, Reverend Samuel Joseph, 10
Mayflower, 81, 99
Melton, Ella L. (Johnson) Davis. *See* Turner, Mrs. Edmund E. [2]
Methodist Chapel, 13
Milne, Reverend Andrew Duncan, 76
Mosher, Flora E., 19
Mosher, Isaac N., 19, 21
Mott, Mrs. John, (née Lucretia Coffin), 95
Munro, Wilfred Harold, 83

N

Neale, Reverend Dr. Rollin Herber, 96
New Bedford, MA, 16
    Frederick Douglass Memorial and Historical Society of New Bedford, 77
    Underground Railroad and, 18, 21, 23, 24
New England Anti-Slavery Society, 16
New England Freedman's Aid Society, 66
New England Magazine, 92
New York Illustrated News, 105
Newby, Dangerfield, 93
Newport, Rhode Island
    anti-slavery and, 15–16
    slave trade in, 2
New-York Tribune, 103

O

Old South Church (Boston, MA), 96
Oliver, Mary, 64–65
Olney, James H., **52**

P

Palmer, Eva J. *See* Adams, Mrs. Edward Stowe [1]
Palmer, General William Jackson, 72
Patten, Mrs. John Frederick, (née Grace Desoe Young), 88
Patton, Mrs. Ludlow, (née Abby Jermima Hutchinson), 36
Pawtucket, R.I.
    Underground Railroad and, 25
Peirce, Captain William, 81
Phillips, Arthur Sherman, xix, 84
Phillips, Wendell, 50, 92, 96, 102, 103, 104, 105, 111, 117
Phillips History of Fall River, xix
Pierce, Palo Alto, 2
Pillsbury, Reverend Parker, 50
Plymouth Colony, 81
Plympton, Mary Elizabeth. *See* Young, Mrs. Reverend Joshua
Potter, Frederick, 61
Providence, R.I.
    anti-slavery and, 16
    Underground Railroad and, 18
Providence and Worcester Railroad, 23

Q

Quaker Meeting House, 60, **64**
Quakers, 5, 15, 17, 18, 60, 65
    practice of buying slave freedom, 3

R

Randolph, Lucretia. *See* Garfield, Mrs. President James Abram
The Religious Society of Friends. *See* Quakers
Reynolds, Elizabeth Mason. *See* Buffinton, Mrs. Oliver
Robert Adams Bookseller and Stationer, 43
Robeson, Andrew, Jr., 17, 18, **42**
    home of (as station on the Underground Railroad), **21**
    letter from, 40
Rodman, Samuel, 16

S

St. Michael's Episcopal Church (Bristol, R.I.), 83
Seeley, Annie M. *See* Turner, Mrs. Edmund E. [1]
Sexton, Sarah J., 12
Sharpes, Fortunates (slave), 3
Siebert, Wilbur Henry, 17, 21
Simmons, Mrs. John Lamport, (née Grace Ruth Thompson), 117
Simpson, Elisha, 31
Simpson, Mrs. Elisha, (née Catharine C. Crank), 29, 31
Slade, Albion King, 26, **28**
    home of (station on the Underground Railroad), 26

Slade, Mrs. Albion King, (née Mary Bridge Canedy), 26, **28**
Slade, Annie Malcolm, 26
Slade, Thomas A., **52**
slave trade, 1–5
  bill of sale of slaves, **3**
  in R.I., 82–83
Slocum, Mark A., 70
Smith, Carrie Maria. *See* Adams, Mrs. Edward Stowe [2]
Smith, Gerrit, 95
Southern Workman, 59
Stevens, Mrs. Daniel, (née Mary Elizabeth Young), 88
Stone Church, 60
Stowe, Mrs. Calvin Ellis. *See* Stowe, Harriet Beecher
Stowe, Harriet Beecher, 40, 50
Stowe, Lydia Ann. *See* Adams, Mrs. Robert
Suckanasset: A History of Falmouth, Massachusetts 1661-1930, 3
Sumner, Charles, 36, 77
Swansea, MA
  Underground Railroad in, 2–3
Swift, John Tuttle, 76

T
Taylor, Stewart, 93
Tea Party Gazette, 45
Temperance movement, 36
Terry, Abby Jane. *See* Lindsey, Mrs. James T.
Thompson, Dauphin Adolphus Osgood, 93
Thompson, Ella J. *See* Towne, Mrs. Francis Newton
Thompson, Elmer Ten, 61
Thompson, Grace Ruth. *See* Simmons, Mrs. John Lamport
Thompson, Henry, 117
Thompson, Mrs. Henry, (née Ruth Brown)
  letter to Reverend Joshua Young, 115–117, **116**
Thompson, Isabella. *See* Brown, Mrs. Watson
Thompson, Mary E., 117
Thompson, William, 93, 103
Thompson, Mrs. William P., (née Mary Elizabeth Brown). *See* Adair, Mrs. Archibald Richard, III
Throop Unitarian Universalist Church (Pasadena, CA), 117
"The Toll House and the East End," 19
Tolman, Mrs. James Pike, (née Mary Elizabeth Chace), 26
Town Hall and Market Building, 36, 51
Town House, 29
Towne, Mrs. Francis Newton, (née Ella J. Thompson), 117
Townsend, James (black slave), 59
Tripp, Azariah Shove, **74**, 75
Truth, Sojourner, xviii, 77, **78**

Tubman, Harriet, 76–77
Turner, Charles Norman, 61
Turner, Edmund E. (black slave), 61, 64
Turner, Mrs. Edmund E. [1], (née Annie M. Seeley), 61
Turner, Mrs. Edmund E. [2], (née Ella L. (Johnson) Davis Melton), 64
Turner, Edward Willard, 61
Turner, Frederick A., 61
Turner, Gertrude L., 61
Turner, Mary Ella, 61
Turner, William, 61
Turner, Mrs. William, (née Matilda Hoge), 61
Tuskegee Institute. *See* Tuskegee University
Tuskegee University, 65
Two Quaker Sisters, 8, 10, 15, 31
Tyndale, Hector, 97

U
Uncle Tom's Cabin, 40, **41**
Underground Railroad, xvii, 24, 25, 26, 76, 88
  history of, 17
  in R.I., 18, 50
  routes of, 21
  stations on the, 3, 18, **18**, 19, **21**, 22, **23**, 26, **32**
  in Swansea, MA, 2–3
The Underground Railroad from Slavery to Freedom, 17
The Underground Railroad in Massachusetts, 21
Unitarian Church, 24, 87, **90**
Unitarian Church (Burlington, VT), 99
Unitarian Society, 10
Usher, Reverend John, 83

V
Valley Falls, R.I., 8, 15, 16, 22, **23**, 25
Van Buren, Martin, 13, 15
Vigilance Committee (Boston, MA), 99
Volter, Frederick, 61

W
Wareham, MA
  Underground Railroad and, 24
Washington, Booker Taliaferro, 65
Webster, Daniel, 32
Weeden, William Babcock, 16
West Newton English and Classical School (Newton, MA), xviii
Westall, Reverend John, 43, 54, **68**, 70
Whigs (political party), 13, 35, 36
White, Isabella (slave), 50–53
White, Maria, 51
White, Solomon, 51
White, Solomon, Jr., 51
Whittier, John Greenleaf, 40
Wide Awakes, 52, 53
Wilbur, Sarah Congdon. *See* Davis, Mrs. Hon. Dr. Robert Thompson

Wilde, Brigadier General Edward Augustus, 75
Wilder, Dr. Daniel, 51
Wilder, Mrs. Dr. Daniel, (née Mary Ann Goss), 51
Williams, Henry, 15
Wood, Leonard, 70
Wood, Nancy L. *See* Hooper, Mrs. Dr. Foster
The Worcester Spy, 118
Wyman, Mrs. John Crawford, (née Elizabeth Buffum "Lillie" Chace), 26

Y

Young, Aaron, 87
Young, Mrs. Aaron, (née Mary Coburn), 87
Young, Grace Desoe. *See* Patten, Mrs. John Frederick
Young, Henry Guy, 88
Young, Mrs. Reverend Joshua, (née Mary Elizabeth Plympton), 87, **89**, **91**
Young, Reverend Joshua, 23–24, **86**, 87–118, **91**
    letter to, 109–112, **110**, 112–114, 115–117
    obituary of, 108–109
Young, Joshua Edson, 88
Young, Lucy Florence, 88
Young, Mary Elizabeth. *See* Stevens, Mrs. Daniel
Young Men's Republican Club of Fall River, **52**

NOTES

NOTES

www.ingramcontent.com/pod-product-compliance
Lightning Source LLC
Chambersburg PA
CBHW071344090426
42738CB00012B/3011